Awesome Automobile Ads

1930s EDITION

Compiled by

Graham Fysh

Cover designed by

Gavin Fysh

Published by LifeTime Creations, Silverdale, Washington
http://www.lifetimecreations.com
Printed in the United States
ISBN: 979-8-9854836-0-4

LIFETIME

These advertisements have been gathered from a variety of publications during the 1930s, including LIFE, TIME, The Saturday Evening Post, Colliers and others.

Contents

1931 ADS

W h e n   a   N a t i o n

This new era of widespread personal power is filling so strange a place in history that even those of us who are thinking about it are baffled most of the time.

We buy an automobile, for example, and plump ourselves down into its soft seats, never realizing that the untold millions of people who have swept through history have lived and died without even the vainest dream of the power that comes to us with the simple turning of a switch and the pressure of a toe.

We are like a nation of kings, each of us on his own throne, behind the wheel of his own power.

★　　★　　★　　★　　★

If you want to get a thrill which will stay with you for the rest of your life, stop your car some time when you are in some far distant land, call one of the peasants in from the field, put him, barefooted, at the wheel, and spend an hour in teaching him to drive. Gradually, as the fear goes out of him and this thing of life comes under his control, you will see his gnarled hands grip the wheel, you'll see his shoulders straighten and a look of awe come into his face that you will never forget.

General Motors

Sits On a Throne

And you will suddenly realize that what you are looking at is the thing that mankind has been striving for through all the centuries—that longing for personal power that has suddenly been fulfilled.

We say quite casually to a friend, "I've just bought a new car." And we get in and drive off without ever a thought of what it means in the history of the world. We swing down the boulevard with a sense of equality and of personal power such as the world in its past has only dreamed of in its wildest dreams.

We have a carriage of wood and steel and beauty beside which any of the old coaches of state seem crude and cumbersome. We have a motor the feel of which transcends any previous sense of power mankind has ever known. And a speed which in any of the old mythologies would have given us the quality of gods instead of men.

And yet, because we live in this strange era, because ours is a part of this new equality of power, because nothing like us has ever happened before, we sum it all up in the casual remark, "I've just bought a new automobile."

GENERAL MOTORS

CHEVROLET • PONTIAC • OLDSMOBILE • OAKLAND • BUICK • LA SALLE • CADILLAC • BODIES BY FISHER

"Mobiloil faalt noo it!"

"Mobiloil faalt noo it!" That's how the Dutch motorist translates to the American motorist his reason for preferring Mobiloil. "Mobiloil stands up!" That's why it is the leading oil throughout the world.

In Holland or Houston

Still strong at the finish—that's stamina!

Whether the trip is 10 miles through hub-deep mud or 1,000 miles over mountains and desert, Mobiloil stands up.

After hardest usage, Mobiloil still fights heat. It still fights wear. It still holds oil pressure. It still stands up.

You can count on the grade of Mobiloil recommended for your car to take all the punishment you can give it.

Push your accelerator down. Let the speedometer swing up—then hold it. Mile after mile, the rugged Mobiloil in your crankcase stands up and protects each moving part, each bearing, each plunging piston.

Mobiloil stands up because it is made to fight heat and wear in your engine. The crude oils from which Mobiloil is made are selected from the world's finest. The most modern refining equipment in existence refines and toughens Mobiloil to give it the supreme power to stand up in your engine.

These are thrifty days. Protect your engine—lengthen its life. You can save real money by always insisting on the oil that stands up—Mobiloil!

We invite you to listen to the Mobiloil Concert, broadcast each Wednesday evening at 8:30, Eastern Daylight Saving Time, from WEAF and 31 associated N. B. C. stations.

Ask here for GARGOYLE Mobiloil

Mobiloil stands up
because it is Made ·· not Found
VACUUM OIL COMPANY

Mobiloil

An enlarged reproduction of the photograph, suitable for framing, will be mailed upon request—Oakland Motor Car Co., 468 Oakland Ave., Pontiac, Mich.

MAKING NEW FRIENDS
AND KEEPING THE OLD

BEAUTY COMES OF INFINITE CARE . . .

You know from your own experience that, without patient care, flowers remain only flowers and vines are just vines. To become a *garden*, they must be guided into a balanced plan of beauty.

To give you beauty in your Oakland and Pontiac cars, we work in the same way. First we build full size working models of plaster. Under searchlights, we study and shape the contours so that lines are pleasing and highlights fall evenly in the right places.

We experiment with fenders and mouldings to develop lines of graceful length. We blend colors until just the right combination is found. We want you to like an Oakland or a Pontiac when you first see it, and be proud of it all the time you drive it.

Every detail is made to work toward a definite scheme of beauty. The new splash aprons are not just added features — they are a part of the car's attractive front-end design. The special rain-gutters, which might have been just rain-gutters, actually improve the body lines. The neat fender lamps seem inseparable from the fenders themselves. Even door handles and hub caps 'fit the picture' perfectly.

Is it worth while — this slow, careful search for beauty? We think so. Just as infinite care makes a garden beautiful, it also makes a car beautiful. And when we see how proud our owners are, we are glad we have taken such pains to please them.

OAKLAND 8   PONTIAC 6

PRODUCTS OF   GENERAL MOTORS

Bodies by   Fisher

SO YOU CAN'T STAND SPEED, MR. WATER-THIN ?
THEN, OUT YOU GO!

You can't "burn up the roads" without burning up Mr. Water-thin. Speed means heat—and heat means the end of that fellow!

Mr. Water-thin is the quart or more of thin, waste oil that ordinary refining leaves in every gallon of motor oil. It's a quart so light-bodied, so quick to vaporize under heat, so useless in a motor, that Quaker State engineers call it "water-thin"—and take no end of care to throw it out!

It is impossible for ordinary refining to remove "water-thin." But Quaker State refining can, and does remove it. Quaker State removes it by a special process which has been installed in every one of Quaker State's refineries —*the most modern refineries in the industry*. This process is a development of Quaker State engineers—a development that was made possible by years of experience and great investments in refining equipment.

Quaker State replaces "water-thin" with rich, heat-fighting lubricant. So Quaker State gives you four full quarts of lubricant to the gallon—instead of three quarts and a quart of waste. You really get an *extra* quart of lubrication. *And that's the reason Quaker State is the world's largest selling Pennsylvania Oil!*

And remember this, too. Quaker State is made entirely from 100% pure Pennsylvania Grade Crude Oil. Quaker State is so free from impurities that it doesn't require acid treatment in refining. That's important! For acids tend to destroy some of an oil's oiliness.

You'll find Quaker State wherever you go. One dealer in every four sells it—and displays the green and white Quaker State sign. It costs 35 cents per quart (slightly more in Canada and at some points in the West) and there's no better bargain in oildom! For in every gallon of Quaker State you get a full *extra* quart of lubrication that battles heat and friction and wear to a fare-you-well!

©1931 QUAKER STATE OIL REFINING CO.

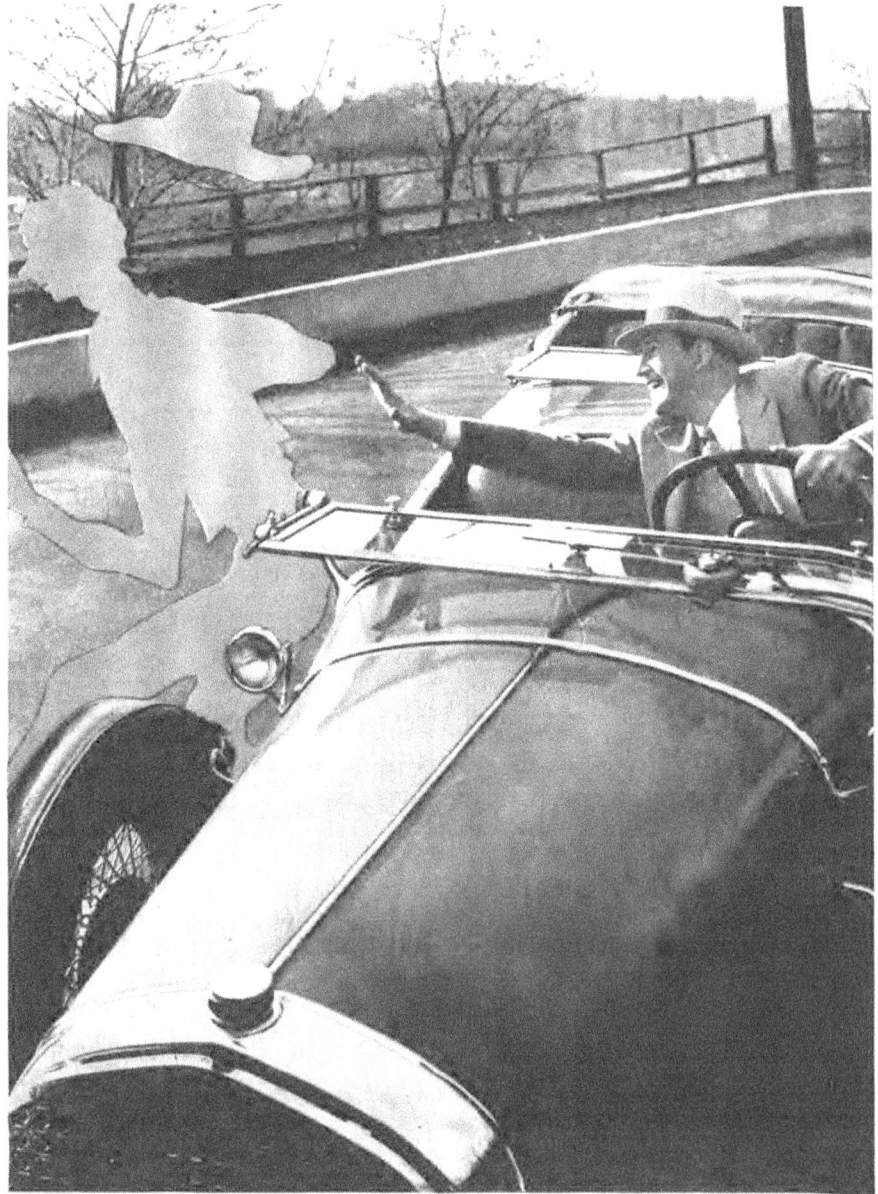

QUAKER STATE
TRADE-MARKS REG. U.S. PAT. 1377.

QUAKER STATE MOTOR OIL CERTIFIED GUARANTEED

LOOK FOR THIS SIGN

MOTOR OIL

THERE'S AN EXTRA QUART
OF LUBRICATION IN EVERY GALLON

Quaker State Oil

Now A SOUND·PROOFED MOTOR CAR

The New Nash has arrived . . . new in line . . . new in beauty . . . new in *silence!*   Body, chassis, motor, transmission, even springs and shock absorbers are silence-engineered, *sound-proofed,* to *permanently* quiet the noise of travel.   Take a *sound-proofed* ride in the New Nash today!

NEW SYNCHRO SAFETY SHIFT PLUS SILENT SECOND NASH

J U S T   A N N O U N C E D   J U N E   T W E N T Y - E I G H T H

WET GAS

slows up any car

dry* TEXACO-ETHYL

speeds up every car

Driving with wet gas is like driving with the choke partly out. The choke floods the manifold — wet gas floods the cylinders. Either way you get sluggish power. No car, once warmed up, will give its best with the choke out — no car, hot or cold, will deliver its utmost with wet gas.

Only a dry* gas can vaporize and burn completely. Texaco-Ethyl is the dry* Ethyl Gasoline. It yields every ounce of its knockless power where you want it — at the cylinders.

Find out for yourself the difference between dry* gas and wet. Today, fill up with dry* Texaco-Ethyl. You will feel a new surge of power and energy that is always yours with dry* Texaco-Ethyl.

THE TEXAS COMPANY
Refiners of a complete line of Texaco Petroleum Products, including Gasoline, Motor Oil, Industrial, Railroad, Marine and Farm Lubricants, Road Asphalts and Asphalt Roofing.

LISTEN

—and for perfect lubrication, use

"CRACK-PROOF"

TEXACO MOTOR OIL
© 1931, The Texas Company

DRY TEXACO **+** ETHYL COMPOUND **=** DRY TEXACO-ETHYL

THERE IS NO BETTER GASOLINE

NOW HE INSISTS ON PURE PENNSYLVANIA

A driver whose name was McFrances
With any old oil would take chances
He just didn't care
Till a bill for repair
Took his coat and his vest and his pantses!

If you are a motorist who accepts any motor oil without question, sooner or later somebody is going to sell you a crankcase full of trouble — sooner or later your motor will get a dose of poor oil. And by the time you find out that a poor oil is poor, it's too late to do anything but pay for the repairs!

So don't take chances. It's easy to be safe. It's easy to make *sure* of the best lubrication your motor can have — by insisting upon motor oil made 100% from Pennsylvania Grade Crude.

Perhaps you are thinking, "But I buy finished motor oil. Why should I be concerned with crude?" A fair question — and here's the answer. Quality starts with the raw material — in a motor oil as in a suit of clothes. And you can write this down as an axiom: the better the crude, the better the finished oil!

Pennsylvania Grade Crude is the finest base for motor oil the world has ever known. Why? Ask Nature. When she made it, she played favorites. She gave it greater oiliness, greater freedom from impurities. She gave it qualities no other oil possesses.

Isn't refining important, too? Certainly, it's important. But nobody has any monopoly on expert refining. In the Pennsylvania field you will find the most advanced refining equipment in the industry. In this — the oldest field — refiners have the longest background of experience. Working with a headstart of the world's best crude, they produce lubricants that are longer-lived, more resistant to heat — lubricants that keep motors running smoothly long after other oils quit. That's why they are chosen for the stiffest lubrication jobs — in automobiles, tractors, airplanes, motorboats; in locomotives, stationary machinery and turbines.

The emblem shown below appears on many brands of finished motor oil. Buy whichever you prefer. Each is made from Pure Pennsylvania Grade Crude. Each will give you safe, thorough, lasting lubrication. FREE! Send for your free copy of one of the most interesting oil booklets ever written. Address the Pennsylvania Grade Crude Oil Association, Dept. C-7, Oil City, Pa.

© 1931, P. G. C. O. A.

This emblem guarantees the quality of the crude oil — the maker's individual brand guarantees the quality of the finished product.

**Guaranteed
100% PURE
PENNSYLVANIA
OIL**
Trade Mark
Reg. U. S. Pat. Off.

PENNSYLVANIA GRADE CRUDE OIL

from which the world's finest motor oils are made

Pennsylvania Oil

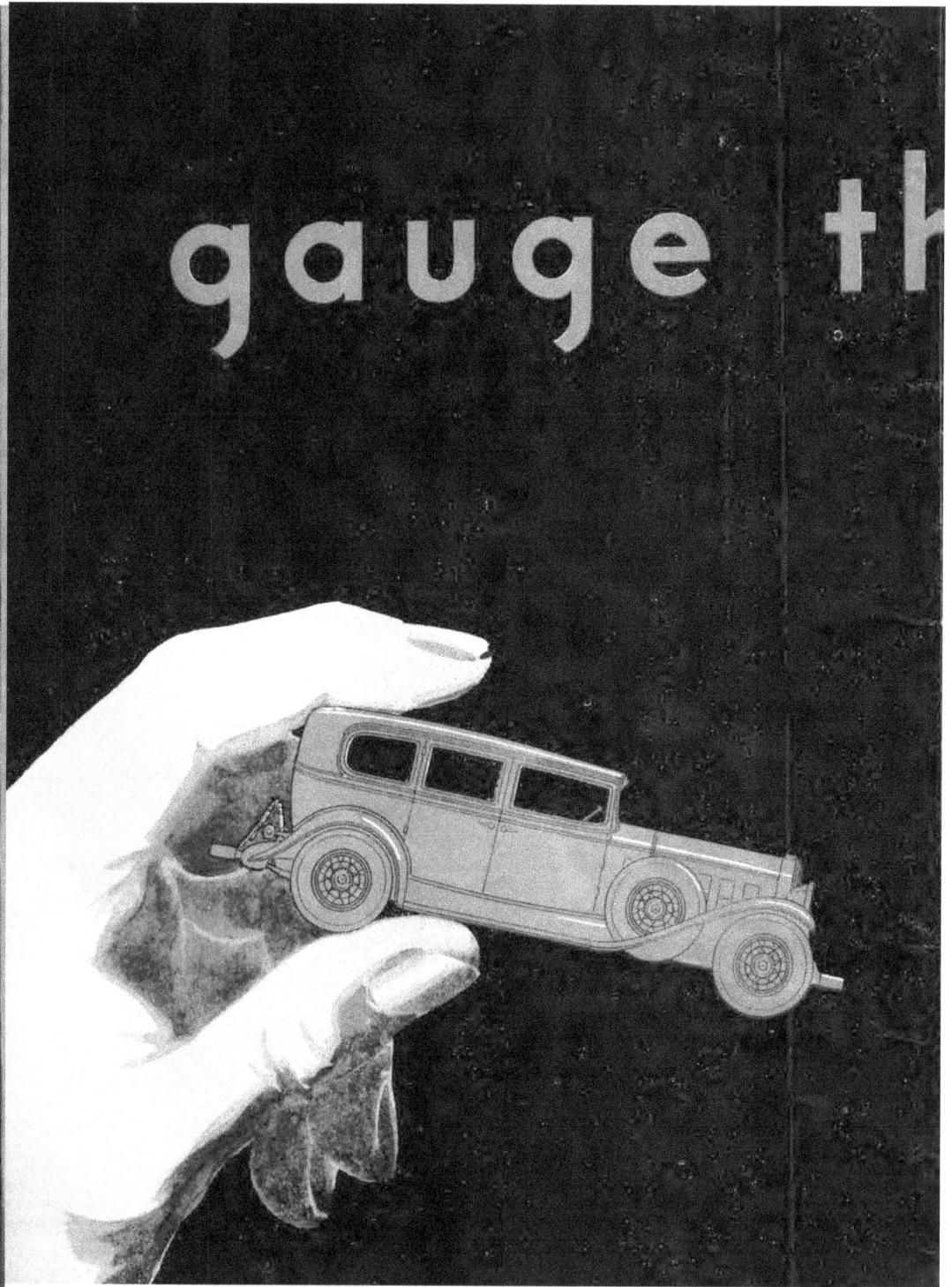

gauge th

In the building of General Motors cars, there is no compromise with standards. If a part fails to conform to specifications, in either substance or dimensions, it is rejected. The General Motors Corporation provides its Divisions with modern plants, up-to-date machinery and equipment, and every known facility for progressive manufacture. Materials, both raw and finished, are obtained from reliable sources, and uniformity in quality is assured through the watchful care of skilled inspectors. Craftsmanship is of high order, tasks are performed with neatness and dispatch, and, wherever possible, savings are effected. Direct results are smooth performance, quietness, dependability, long life and unusually low prices. Sound manufacturing is a General Motors fundamental and is clearly reflected in the outstanding values of General Motors cars.

GM

GENERAL MOTORS

General Motors

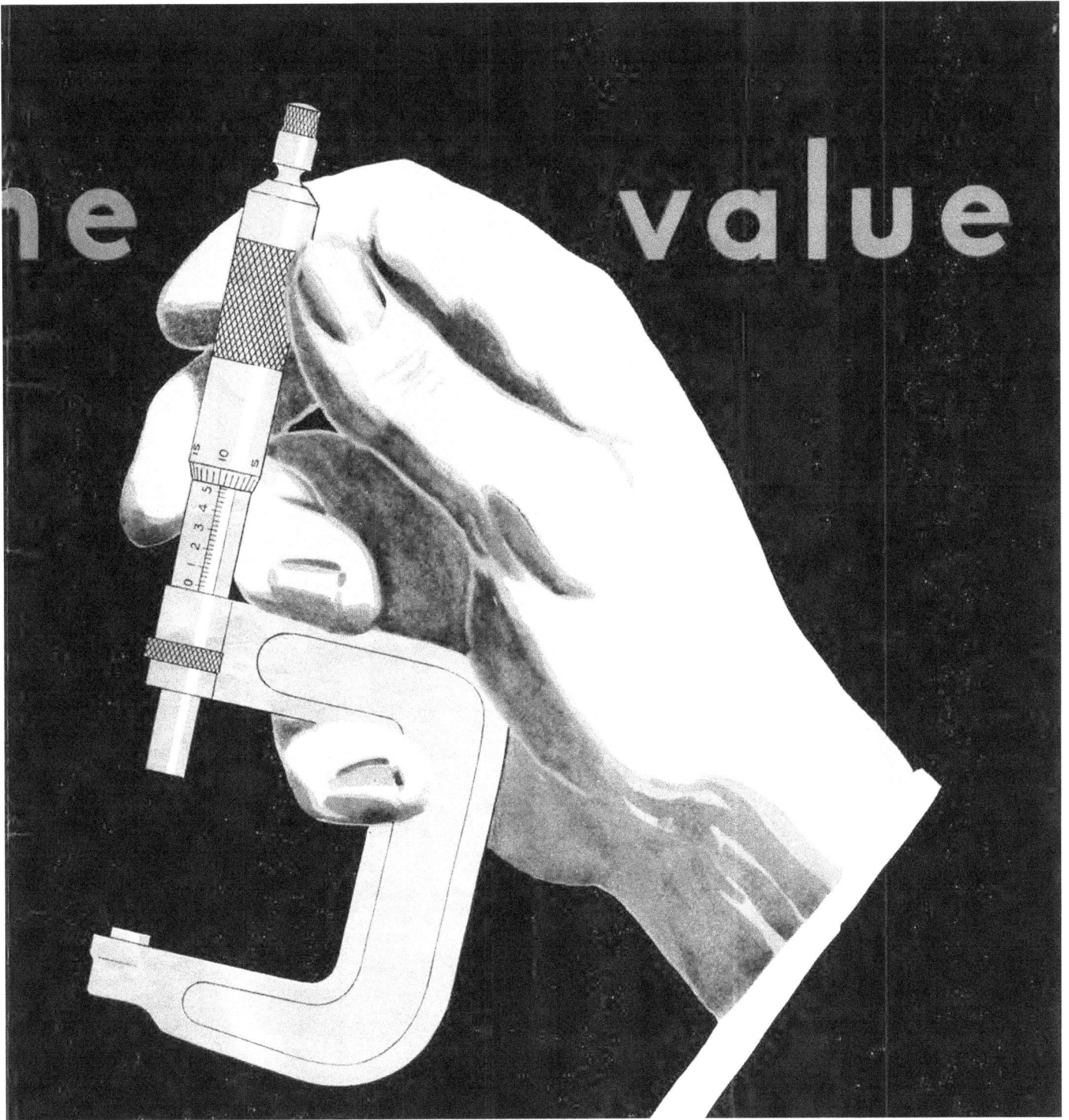

GENERAL MOTORS CARS
HAVE OUTSTANDING VALUE

CHEVROLET · PONTIAC · OLDSMOBILE · OAKLAND · BUICK · LA SALLE · CADILLAC · BODIES BY FISHER

MOTORISTS WISE
SIMONIZ
TRADE MARK REG. ... AT. OFF.

Every car NEEDS SIMONIZ

Why Every Car Should Be SIMONIZED

1 Restores the beauty

2 Protects the finish and makes it last longer

3 Keeps colors from fading

4 Saves time and money

Simoniz guards the finish from weather, dirt and grime that otherwise dull and destroy its beauty. That's why the sooner any car is Simonized the better.

And nothing takes the place of Simoniz for protecting the finish. It keeps a car beautiful for years. Makes the finish last longer, and keeps colors from fading.

Simonizing a car is easy. If your car is dulled and discolored, use the wonderful Simoniz Kleener first. It quickly restores the beauty of the finish by removing all grime, stains, and blemishes. Then Simoniz gives lasting protection.

After a car is Simonized dust or dirt can be wiped off with just a dry cloth and the finish sparkles bright as ever.

Be good to your car. Insist on Simoniz and Simoniz Kleener — for Simonizing is the secret of lasting motorcar beauty. Sold at leading hardware, auto accessory stores, and garages everywhere.

THE SIMONIZ COMPANY, CHICAGO, U.S.A.

Simoniz car polish

1½-Ton 131-inch Stake Truck—Price including body $710, dual wheels optional $25 extra. With 157" wheelbase $810. Dual wheels standard.

Sedan Delivery—Unusually spacious and good-looking body by Fisher. Deep, wide rear openings. Wire wheels. Price $575.

1½-Ton Panel Truck—Disc wheels standard. Price including body $760. With half-ton chassis $555. Disc wheels.

1½-Ton 131-inch High and Wide Express Truck—Price including body $715. Dual wheels $25 extra. With 157" wheelbase $800. Dual wheels standard.

1½-Ton 131-inch Stock Rack Truck—Price including body $730. Dual wheels optional $25 extra. With 157" wheelbase $830. Dual wheels standard equipment.

LEADING AMERICAN BUSINESSES RELY ON CHEVROLET SIX-CYLINDER TRUCKS

Among America's foremost business institutions, there is a definite swing toward Chevrolet six-cylinder trucks. Everywhere, you see evidence of this: Chevrolet stake trucks at some famous packer's warehouse. Chevrolet express trucks parked in the yards of a leading manufacturer. Scores of other Chevrolet models, on the roads daily, bearing the name of a big oil firm—a grocery chain—a great public utility.

This growing preference for Chevrolet—among large fleet owners—is especially significant. For, after all, the man who buys one or two trucks wants exactly the same thing in hauling equipment as the big national concern.

Capacity, for instance. Chevrolet's frame has the length, the strength and the support to accommodate bodies of maximum load capacity—to carry big, heavy pay-loads, and reduce the number of trips per job. **Stamina and durability.** The Chevrolet chassis has a heavy-duty clutch, a rugged rear axle, big brakes, and a massive frame—for long, dependable service, without delays for repair. **Power and speed.** The Chevrolet 50-horsepower six-cylinder engine and the 4-speed transmission provide ample power to haul full-capacity loads at modern road-speeds. **Year 'round economy.** Chevrolet first-cost is one of the lowest in the market. And many firms find that the Chevrolet truck costs less to operate than any other they have ever used.

It's always wise, in choosing a truck, to be guided by the judgment of large fleet operators. Leading American business firms have made a careful, scientific analysis of trucks and truck costs. And they are purchasing more and more six-cylinder Chevrolet trucks every day!

CHEVROLET 1½-TON CHASSIS WITH 131-INCH WHEELBASE (Dual wheels optional $25 extra) **$520**

1½-TON CHASSIS WITH 157-INCH WHEELBASE (Dual wheels standard) . . $590
COMMERCIAL CHASSIS $355

All chassis prices f. o. b. Flint, Michigan. All truck body prices f. o. b. Indianapolis, Ind. Special equipment extra.

CHEVROLET SIX CYLINDER TRUCKS
« FOR LOWEST TRANSPORTATION COST »

Chevrolet Trucks

The Better Performance of CHAMPIONS Speaks for Itself . . .

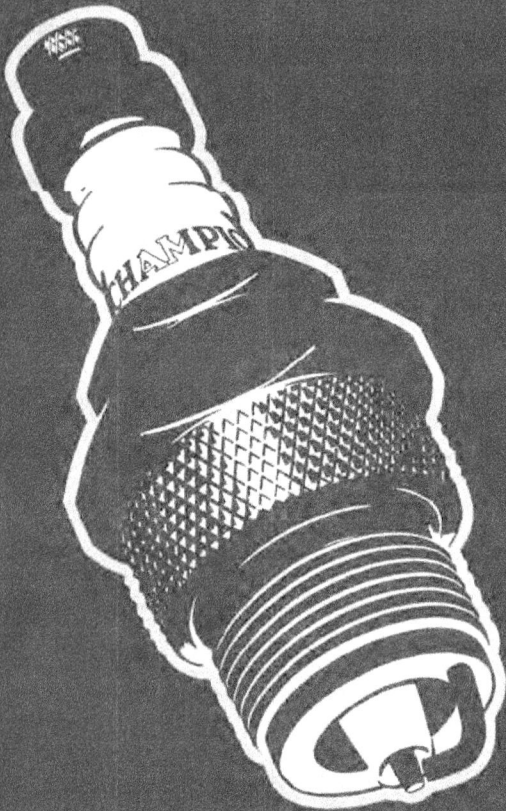

THE merit of any product is accurately measured by the public's acceptance of that product . . . Champion Spark Plugs have long enjoyed the proud privilege of excelling and outselling throughout the world, because with them every engine becomes a better performing engine . . . Install a set of the new improved Champions in your car now. Their better performance is a reality which speaks eloquently for itself.

CHAMPION SPARK PLUG COMPANY, TOLEDO, OHIO; WINDSOR, ONTARIO

CHAMPION
Spark plugs

CHANGE SPARK PLUGS EVERY 10,000 MILES FOR BETTER ENGINE PERFORMANCE

The New and Improved Champion Spark Plugs have a definitely increased range of spark plug efficiency and they make every engine a better performing engine. Better in power and flexibility. Better in starting, idling, and at top speed . . . Install a set in your car now

Champion spark plugs

NEW KIND OF AUTO EYES

Makes Night Driving Safer Than Day!

No more headlight glare! No more driving "blind" on a crowded highway at night! An astonishing new invention permits every auto owner to see perfectly at night. Banishes night wrecks and smash-ups. Ends fear of running over children or animals. Makes night driving actually easier and safer than day driving. Now backed by a two million dollar corporation that guarantees it to do everything claimed here or it costs you absolutely nothing. Simply mail coupon for the manufacturer's liberal Free Test Offer.

Fits Any Headlight
Ends Dangerous Dimming
Doubles Road Light!

This new kind of Light even LOOKS entirely different. No wonder every installation brings a dozen more sales.

Lights up entire roadway including ditches at side. Gives perfect illumination without shadows or flickering.

Banishes Glare Shields, Spot-lights, etc. Floods the road with light yet absolutely cannot glare.

AT Last! An amazingly queer yet simple invention lifts the bane and curse of night driving from the motoring world. Actually like magic this altogether new discovery replaces the "bulbs" in automobile headlights with truly amazing results. Road illumination is instantly doubled, yet glare is absolutely banished. Ordinary objects in the road, ruts, animals, obstructions, etc., are made clearly visible at least **three** times as far. This new kind of light even cuts right through fog, mist, rain and snow in which ordinary lights are next to useless. Gives you a solid wall of light 3 feet high, 25 to 30 feet wide. Instead of ordinary "direct" light, this beam is composed entirely of double-reflected or "infused" light. This new kind of beam pours down the highway ahead of you so far that you can actually see to go 70 miles an hour in safety. At a 40 to 50 mile an hour clip, it is positively safer than daylight because all the light is on the road and you see nothing of your surroundings to distract you. No wonder motorists simply go wild over this discovery wherever it is introduced!

INEXPENSIVE

Patent rights in this new lighting invention are fully protected. It is not in any sense a new "attachment." There is no wiring or installation. No extra upkeep.

In the past, millions of motorists have paid from $10 to $25 for so-called spot-lights and driving-lights that at best are only makeshifts. This new exclusive method costs only a fraction as much and actually doubles road illumination with your present headlights! Banishes the need for glare shields. Cuts through the other fellow's light so you can see the road, yet absolutely cannot glare in his eyes. No wonder fleet owners, manufacturers, taxi and bus lines, etc., concerns like Blue & Gray Bus Lines, W.Va.; Wallace & Tiernan, N. J.; Columbus Fire Trucks, etc., are fast turning to this discovery as standard equipment. It's positively needed on every car in America new or old **right this minute.**

OFFERED ON INTRODUCTORY TEST

Space here limits further discussion of the facts about this discovery. Every driver who ever rolled half-blind down the highway at night knows exactly what such an invention means in added speed, nervous energy saved, perhaps fatal accidents banished. To prove as quickly as possible to motorists in every section what this invention will do, the manufacturer now offers a set to every motorist on FREE TEST OFFER. Simply mail the coupon for details. No obligation. Send it today.

Agent Makes $1,400 in One Week

Full-time and spare-time workers. New FREE DEMONSTRATION Plan with SALES GUARANTEED. EXCLUSIVE TERRITORY. Get in on ground floor. Sell in bunches to fleet owners. A real chance for $8 to $14 very first hour; $6,000 to $10,000 a year. Wehner of Pennsylvania made $1,125 in 90 days' spare time; Owens of W. Va. made over $500 a month; Davis of Pennsylvania made $1,400 in one week. No limit for distributors. Use coupon for Free Test Offer and get full details of money-making proposition. WRITE QUICK! It's red-hot! Going big!

HACHMEISTER-LIND CO.,
Established 1903
DEPT. M-270   PITTSBURGH, PA.

Hachmeister-Lind Co., Dept. M-270,
Pittsburgh, Pa.
    Rush details of your Free Test Offer and facts about agent's money-making opportunities, without obligation.

Name

Address

Town   State

Auto Eyes headlights

SPEED BLEND

FROM DU PONT, *MAKER OF DUCO*

CARE WILL SAVE YOUR CAR

Try this NEW fast-working No. 7 Duco Polish

STANDS TO REASON, doesn't it, that the chemists who created the famous Duco finish for today's automobiles should also create the best polish for keeping that finish clean and bright?

SPEED BLEND is a fast-working cleaner and polish. It disposes of Traffic Film* with magical ease. Your car gleams again as on the day it was new. Save time and effort with SPEED BLEND. Save the car finish, too. No acids or grit in SPEED BLEND; it's *safe* as well as speedy. Whether you personally polish your car or have it done at a garage or polishing station, insist upon this NEW No. 7 Duco Polish.

TRAFFIC FILM—Oily, sticky dust and grime, baked by the sun into a hard film which soap and water can't remove. Speed Blend takes it off—quickly—easily—safely.

CARE WILL SAVE YOUR CAR

STOP RUST-CHOKE!
Clean out rust and scale from your engine cooling system with No. 7 Radiator Cleaner. You'll be amazed at the increased power, better engine performance.

KEEP BRIGHT-NESS BRIGHT
with No. 7 Nickel Polish for radiator, lamps and hardware.

QUICK CURE FOR WORN SPOTS!
Touch up worn places and scratches on fenders, bumpers, tire carriers, etc., with du Pont No. 7 Touch-up Black. Brush supplied in can.

PRESERVE THE LUSTRE!
After polishing car, use du Pont No. 7 Super-Lustre Cream to preserve gloss and protect finish against weathering. Much easier to use than ordinary waxes.

SAVE THE TOP!
Restore the lustre, waterproof the top with No. 7 Auto Top Finish. You can brush it on in half an hour. It dries overnight. No. 7 is made by du Pont, the world's leading maker of auto top materials.

Send Coupon — Get Beauty Kit

Containing generous samples of (1) No. 7 Duco Polish, (2) No. 7 Super-Lustre Cream, and (3) No. 7 Auto Top Finish. Enclose 10 cents to help cover postage.

E. I. DU PONT DE NEMOURS & CO., INC., Desk C6
General Motors Building, DETROIT, MICH.
Canadian Industries Limited, P & V Div., Toronto 9, Canada

Send me your Sample Beauty Kit for my auto. I am enclosing 10 cents (coin or stamps) to help pay the mailing cost. (*Good only in U. S. and Canada*.)

NAME
ADDRESS
CITY   STATE

Speed Blend car polish

International
Quality Trucks
—in the low price range!

New Model A-2, a 1½-ton 4-speed International. The price of the 136-inch wheelbase chassis with standard equipment is

$675
f. o. b. factory

IN the building of high-grade motor trucks, International Harvester has advanced by what may well be called "leaps and bounds." Today this Company ranks high among the leaders in truck manufacture, making both speed and heavy-duty models for all hauling requirements. Three-fourths of the huge annual output of International Trucks is sold to industry and commerce, one-fourth to agriculture.

International Truck success is based on true quality, demonstrated economy and lasting satisfaction—and on SERVICE.

The largest Company-owned truck service organization in the world stands back of International Truck operation. Branches at 183 points in the United States and Canada, supplemented by thousands of dealers, provide a service that is of extreme value to the International owner. Whether he is in

Syracuse or San Diego, in Seattle or Savannah, the same complete stocks, the same modern equipment for repairs and overhauling, the same expert attention at lowest costs are at his service at a neighboring International branch.

TODAY's official new-truck registration figures indicate that International is increasing its leadership in truck manufacture and sales during 1931—growing tribute to these trucks and this service.

The full line of modern International trucks, of handsome design, and with absolutely no sacrifice in quality, is now available with a low schedule of prices made possible by quantity production.

Ask for a demonstration of the 1½-ton Model A-2 featured above, or any other International. Sizes range from ¾-ton to 5-ton.

INTERNATIONAL HARVESTER COMPANY
606 S. Michigan Ave. OF AMERICA (INCORPORATED) Chicago, Illinois

BALTIMORE *or* BAKERSFIELD

International branches are established *to stay*. We may relocate to better the service, but we have never abandoned a territory. A view of the interior of one factory-standard service branch, in small town or large, is a view into them all— 183 *Company-owned International branches*. And in-between are *thousands of International Truck dealers*, with service ideals patterned after our own. The object of them all is to keep Internationals on the job at low cost — to keep International owners content with their trucks.

A typical International Branch—Baltimore, Md.

The International Dealer (A. H. Karpe) at Bakersfield, Calif.

INTERNATIONAL TRUCKS

International Trucks

BUILT TO ENDURE

Sturdy, masterly construction makes Prest-O-Lite Batteries last longer, go further, give more satisfaction. Ask your dealer to point out the many superior Prest-O-Lite Battery features.

● *Prest-O-Lite Prices Were Never So Low* ●

Prest-O-Lite

Prest-O-Lite Storage Battery Sales Corporation
(Associated with The Electric Auto-Lite Company)
Oakland, Cal.   INDIANAPOLIS, IND.   Toronto, Canada

Prest-O-Lite Battery

MAKING NEW FRIENDS
AND KEEPING THE OLD

GOOD CROPS DEPEND ON GOOD SEED

Ambitious farm boys, as they help to till the soil, learn first of all that only selected seed can grow the choicest crop. Much the same thing is true of building a barn, constructing a road, or making an automobile . . . the materials we start with largely govern our success.

We have searched the world over for the right materials for our cars. For instance, we have found that the best material for cylinder blocks is an alloy containing a rare type of iron obtainable only in a remote section of the Province of Oriente on the northeast coast of Cuba. In the original ore—called Mayari ore—nature has combined certain proportions of nickel, chromium, vanadium and titanium which no man has ever been able to duplicate.

Using this iron, we are enabled to make cylinder block cast-

ings with nearly twice the usual strength. The ore costs us a great deal more, but with it we can make our cylinder walls of such even texture that they take a glass-like finish. They last much longer, and hold a higher compression all through their life. Thus the motors in Oaklands and Pontiacs gain in both durability and performance.

And so it is with many other materials that go into these cars . . . we get piston electro-plating materials from Malaya; chromium from British South Africa and Portuguese East Africa; cadmium for rust-proofing from Australia and Transylvania; and antimony for Babbitt metal from Bolivia and China.

But if results interest you more than causes, will you drive one of these two fine cars? Learn the extra measure of value they offer through careful choosing of materials.

OAKLAND 8  PONTIAC 6

PRODUCTS OF   GENERAL MOTORS

Bodies by   Fisher

General Motors   Pontiac 6   Oakland 8

A Strange New Epoch

The world has seen more than forty million automobiles roll through its highways and byways in a little over thirty years. In this country we have over twenty-three million cars in use today.

Here in America, we are apt to attribute our large part in this development to our money, our manufacturing capacity, or our genius for invention. Important factors, of course. But the real reason lies deeper than any of these.

The real reason is that the peoples of the earth had come to understand that individual personal power is the highest achievement of man. And the automobile gave them the greatest feeling of that individual personal power.

Nothing else could account for these millions upon millions of automobiles—especially for the millions of cars which have been put within the range of every man and have given him that sense of personal power and equality for which he has been striving so long.

For he can look out from any automobile he may own, even at the

General Motors

of   Personal   Power

costliest turnouts on the avenue, and know that his motor is part of this
strange new source of power; that the conveyance in which he is riding has
more of comfort and luxury than any vehicle, great or small, ever con-
structed for the open roads before; that under his own direction and
control he will be able to travel farther than the most of mankind has
ever traveled before, and faster than his own laws of safety will allow.

Seated in whatever automobile he may happen to own, his sense of
personal power and rightful equality is complete. Naturally, a man's
personal preference keeps calling for finer cars and more tangible values,
but this is only a human desire. When he gets into any automobile, his
age-old longing for personal power has found its response at last.

So the forty million automobiles in thirty years is not so hard to understand when you come at it in this way. Nor is it hard to see why
every man and woman wants one, nor why every member of the family
wants one, too.

G E N E R A L   M O T O R S

CHEVROLET · PONTIAC · OLDSMOBILE · OAKLAND · BUICK · LA SALLE · CADILLAC · BODIES BY FISHER

The BOSCH
ROBERT BOSCH A. G.

Pyro-Action

SPARK PLUG

IS A BETTER PLUG AND GIVES BETTER PERFORMANCE

YOU CAN PROVE THIS BY INSTALLING A SET TODAY

SOLD BY

UNITED AMERICAN BOSCH CORPORATION
SPRINGFIELD   MASSACHUSETTS

BRANCHES – NEW YORK · DETROIT · CHICAGO · SAN FRANCISCO
CANADIAN WAREHOUSE: TORONTO, CANADA. SPARK PLUG PRICES SAME AS IN U.S.

Bosch Spark Plugs

Scamper up hills
with **ETHYL**

Rocky Mountain sheep have the nimble vigor Ethyl
gives motors on hills. Not that Ethyl Gasoline doesn't
make cars run better on level roads; it does. But you
ought to try it on hills. There's where controlled com-
bustion gets a full chance to prove its value (and
saving). The Ethyl fluid in Ethyl Gasoline prevents un-
even explosions that cause power-waste, harmful
"knock" and overheating; changes them to smooth,
propelling strokes of power that bring out the best in
any motor. Ethyl Gasoline Corporation, New York City.

*The active ingredient used in Ethyl
fluid is lead.*

ETHYL GASOLINE

Ethyl Gasoline

Try SPEED BLEND
on your car today

Restore the lustre with this new, fast-working No. 7 Duco Polish... made by du Pont

GET a can of SPEED BLEND from your dealer. Pour a little of this new, fast-working cleaner and polish on a cloth and rub it on the dull, drab surface of your car. Then wipe it off with a dry, clean cloth, and stand back and admire your handiwork. Traffic Film* is gone. Your car gleams again as on the day it was new. Note how little time and effort this transformation takes. SPEED BLEND is safe, too—it has no acids or grit to wear away the car finish. Insist upon SPEED BLEND. Du Pont, who created Duco, makes this NEW fast-working No. 7 Duco Polish, and recommends it for your car.

STOP RUST CHOKE!
Clean out rust and scale with No. 7 Radiator Cleaner. More power, better engine performance.

QUICK CURE FOR WORN SPOTS!
Touch up worn places and scratches on fenders, bumpers, tire carriers, etc., with du Pont No. 7 Touch-up Black Brush supplied in can.

KEEP BRIGHTNESS BRIGHT!
with No. 7 Nickel Polish for radiator, lamps and hardware. Made by du Pont.

SAVE THE TOP!
Restore the lustre, waterproof the top with No. 7 Auto Top Finish. You can brush it on in half an hour. It dries overnight. No. 7 is made by du Pont, the world's leading maker of auto top materials.

WAX THE FINISH!
After polishing car, use du Pont No. 7 Super-Lustre Cream to preserve gloss and protect finish against weathering. Much easier to use than ordinary waxes.

*TRAFFIC FILM—Oily, sticky dust and grime, baked by the sun into a hard film which soap and water can't remove. Speed Blend takes it off—quickly—easily—safely.

CARE WILL SAVE YOUR CAR

SEND COUPON – GET BEAUTY KIT
Containing generous samples of (1) No. 7 Duco Polish, (2) No. 7 Super-Lustre Cream, and (3) No. 7 Auto Top Finish. Enclose 10 cents to help cover postage.

• • •

E. I. DU PONT DE NEMOURS & CO., INC., Desk C9, General Motors Bldg., DETROIT, MICHIGAN
Canadian Industries Ltd., P&V Div., Toronto 9, Canada

Send me your Sample Beauty Kit for my auto. I am enclosing 10 cents (coin or stamps) to help pay the mailing cost. (*Good only in U. S. and Canada.*)

NAME_____

ADDRESS_____

CITY_____ STATE_____

Speed Blend car polish

1933 ADS

MOTORISTS WISE
SIMONIZ

This Lincoln Coupe has gone over 97,000 miles. It still looks new because Simoniz protected its finish always. The owner of this car is Mr. A. L. Doering—"Doering Spark Plugs"—New York City

Beauty Mileage

9 7 5 6 2
2 7 0

● *There's*
Nothing Like
SIMONIZ
FOR KEEPING CARS BEAUTIFUL

Think of it! . . . Simoniz will make your car look new again! And then it will keep it beautiful year after year —always, in fact!

Millions Simoniz their cars. And you should, too! Every car, new or old, absolutely needs Simoniz. It stops weather and dirt from dulling and ruining the finish, positively makes it last longer and keeps the colors from fading.

Nothing compares with Simoniz. It's different from so-called waxes and polishes that give but a temporary shine.

Simoniz gives beauty that *lasts!* Dust and dirt don't stick to a Simonized finish. A soft cloth wipes them off in a second—so that you can keep your car sparkling bright without bother or expense.

Simonizing is easy to do. The wonderful Simoniz Kleener quickly and safely removes all grime, discolorations and film, restores the original lustre *without* hard rubbing. Then Simoniz keeps your car looking new month after month no matter where you go or in what kind of weather you drive!

●

Always insist on Simoniz and Simoniz Kleener. Nothing takes their place. These famous products are NEVER sold under any other name. See that you get what you ask for. Sold at hardware and accessory stores everywhere!

THE SIMONIZ COMPANY, CHICAGO, U.S.A.

Simoniz car polish

Long Distance .... *in telephone service you pay for the extra miles...but with* TEMPERED RUBBER *you get extra mileage at no extra cost*

Only U.S. *builds* TIRES *with* TEMPERED RUBBER

TEMPERED RUBBER, developed and used only by U. S., is tougher, longer lasting than any other. It wears down slower, prolongs tire life, materially lengthens the tire's measure of safety. Look for the words Tempered Rubber on the sidewall; it pays to make sure.

United States Rubber Company
WORLD'S LARGEST PRODUCER OF RUBBER

Tempered Rubber

BULLETIN!

DON'T LET THIS
HAPPEN TO YOU
...INSIST ON A
"HOT PATCH"
TUBE REPAIR

•

Shaler
Nation - Wide
Tire and Tube
Repair Service

•

TRAGEDY
they call it

but we wonder if it isn't
CARELESSNESS!

Almost every day you read it in the papers
"Five people injured in a triple collision" . .
or something similar . . . Tragedy? . . . Perhaps
. . but we wonder if it isn't carelessness.
Accidents due in part or in whole to
faulty tube repairs are "preventable".

Don't let carelessness turn your motoring into tragedy. Insist on a "Hot Patch"
tube repair . . *the repair that becomes
part of the tube* . . Safe . . dependable
. . unconditionally guaranteed . . From
coast to coast this famous "Hot Patch"
method is used by all "Authorized Mem-
bers" of the Shaler Nation-Wide Tire
and Tube Repair Service. Let a man who
knows how repair your tubes. Look for
the identification sign in your neighborhood. Play Safe! Hot Patches cost no
more than ordinary repairs.

Sponsored by
THE SHALER COMPANY
Milwaukee and Waupun, Wisconsin

**Let a man who
KNOWS HOW
repair your tubes**

85,000 Stations are ready to
serve you from Coast to
Coast. Also available in
Associated, Barnsdall, Magnolia, Phillips, Shell and
stations operated by many
other nationally known Oil
Companies. Look for the Authorized Membership Sign!

THE SHALER CO., Milwaukee, Wis.
Please send booklet checked below
☐ 958 For Car Owners
☐ 551 For Dealers

SHALER
NATION-WIDE REPAIR SERVICE

Shaler Repair Service

LESS THAN $1.50 A MONTH
FOR TWELVE MONTHS
GIVES YOU
SUPER SAFETY GLASS PROTECTION

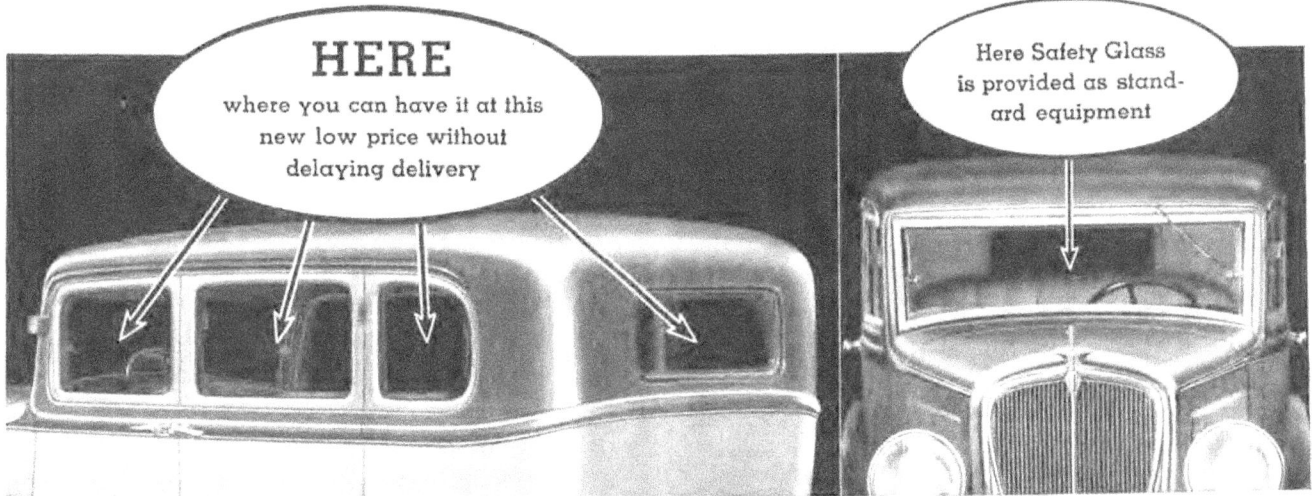

HERE
where you can have it at this new low price without delaying delivery

Here Safety Glass is provided as standard equipment

For less than $1.50 more on each of twelve monthly payments, you can now have L-O-F super Safety Glass in *all windows* of your new car, when it is not already furnished there free of charge by the manufacturer. That's where you *must* have it, in order to provide the greatest available protection. Safety Glass in the windshield alone is not sufficient. Windows, too, are liable to break and injure passengers.

DO THIS
WHEN YOU BUY A CAR

Ask the salesman where the Safety Glass is and just how much there is of it. Now that Safety Glass *all around* costs so very little,

can you afford to buy a new car without this essential safeguard in *all windows* as well as in the windshield? Can you safely drive a car without it? Safety Glass all around is the only way to be sure you are protecting yourself and your family to the fullest possible extent against broken, flying glass.

In Packard, Studebaker, Franklin, Reo Royale, Ford De Luxe Models, Cadillac, La Salle, Lincoln and Buick 80 and 90, Libbey-Owens-Ford super Safety Glass is supplied in both windshields and windows at no extra charge.

In Graham, Reo Flying Cloud, Willys, Ford Standard Models, Buick 50 and 60, Chevrolet,

Oldsmobile, Pontiac, Rockne, Auburn and Cord, it is supplied in windshields at no extra charge. You can have it in the windows at a new low price, without delaying delivery.

LIBBEY-OWENS-FORD GLASS CO., Toledo, Ohio

Our authorized replacement dealers will quote you prices on super Safety Glass specially fitted to the windshield or windows of your present car. Ask the L-O-F distributor, who is listed in the "Where To Buy It" section of your local telephone directory, for name of nearest dealer.

LIBBEY · OWENS · FORD
SAFETY GLASS
FOR LASTING CLEARNESS AND GREATER SAFETY

Libbey-Owens-Ford Safety Glass

NEW Beauty Treatment FOR YOUR CAR !

1. First, you apply the new cleaner, after car is washed and dry. Cleaner dries to a white powder, easily removed with a cloth. What a wonderful transformation! And so easy to use!

2. Next, you apply protective coat of the new wax. Takes about one-half former waxing time. Shields the finish against wear and weather — gives a lasting, rich, beautiful polish.

AMAZING NEW WAX METHOD !

Restores lost beauty! Do the job yourself—in half the usual time—very little cost! Send coupon.

From carowners everywhere come glowing letters of praise for this new beauty treatment for automobiles. "We've used every kind of cleaner and polish on the market, but this beats them all!"—so letters read. • You can try this method on your own car so easily! Your dealer has a special combination offer (free polishing cloth) ready for you. Or send in coupon below and test these products at practically no expense.

This amazing wax method, developed in the famous Johnson Wax Laboratories, actually restores the lost beauty of your car—and gives you an easy method for maintaining and protecting that beauty —whether your car is new or old • You can do the work yourself—with half the usual time and effort—and at very little cost. Reduces car washings greatly, and adds $50 to $200 to trade-in value.

The method employs two new products. The *first* is **Johnson's Auto Cleaner**—an entirely new kind of cleaner. Easily applied, dries to a white powder that is quickly wiped off with a cloth, taking dirt, scum, road film and dullness with it —*without marring the surface.* • The *second* is **Johnson's New Auto Wax**— that maintains and protects the finish against sun, weather, road dirt. Takes one half the usual time and effort—and the cost is negligible. One waxing costs 7 cents. Dust slides off the wax. Rain doesn't get through. Occasional waxing maintains the beauty — and between times rubbing with a cloth keeps the car gleaming.

FREE POLISHING CLOTH

For limited time, a bolt of polishing cloth is being given free with every purchase of both products. Cleaner sells for 25c, pint size. Wax is 35c, enough for 7 waxings. Combination price $1.15, polishing cloth free. At hardware, drug, grocery and department stores — auto supply stores and service stations.

JOHNSON'S ❶ AUTO CLEANER ❷ AUTO WAX

Get a trial can of each at the nearest ten cent store. If not in stock, mail this coupon. S. C. Johnson & Son, Inc., Dept. G5, Racine, Wis. Please send me a generous trial can of both the new Johnson's Auto Cleaner and Johnson's Auto Wax. I enclose 10c to cover postage for both.

Name

Address in full

Johnson's auto wax

1935 ADS

"Of all things....

I've been shopping for gasoline

I buy nearly 600 gallons a year... *if there's any difference between gasolines, I want to know it!*

This morning I decided to do something I'd never done before. I asked five different gasoline stations about their gasoline. I finally bought Texaco Fire-Chief after talking to the man there.

he told me: That Fire-Chief Gasoline had originally been developed in the Texaco laboratories as a gasoline for emergency use in fire engines, ambulances, etc.

he told me: That Fire-Chief was used by many of the cross-country bus lines who have to have low mileage costs. Among the bus companies that he mentioned was the Greyhound Bus Company.

he told me: That Fire-Chief is sold in all 48 States. It seems that tourists, by demanding Texaco Gasoline as they drove across the country, carried it into every State.

he told me: That uniformly good performance is very desirable in gasoline. One of the advantages he pointed out in Texaco is that it always gives the same good performance — no matter where you buy it.

he *sold* me!"

TEXACO (T) TEXACO FIRE-CHIEF

Tune in on "Jumbo"
DIRECT FROM NEW YORK HIPPODROME

THE NEW FIRE-CHIEF PROGRAM
TUESDAY NIGHTS 9:30 E. S. T.
COAST-TO-COAST · · · N. B. C.

Texaco gasoline

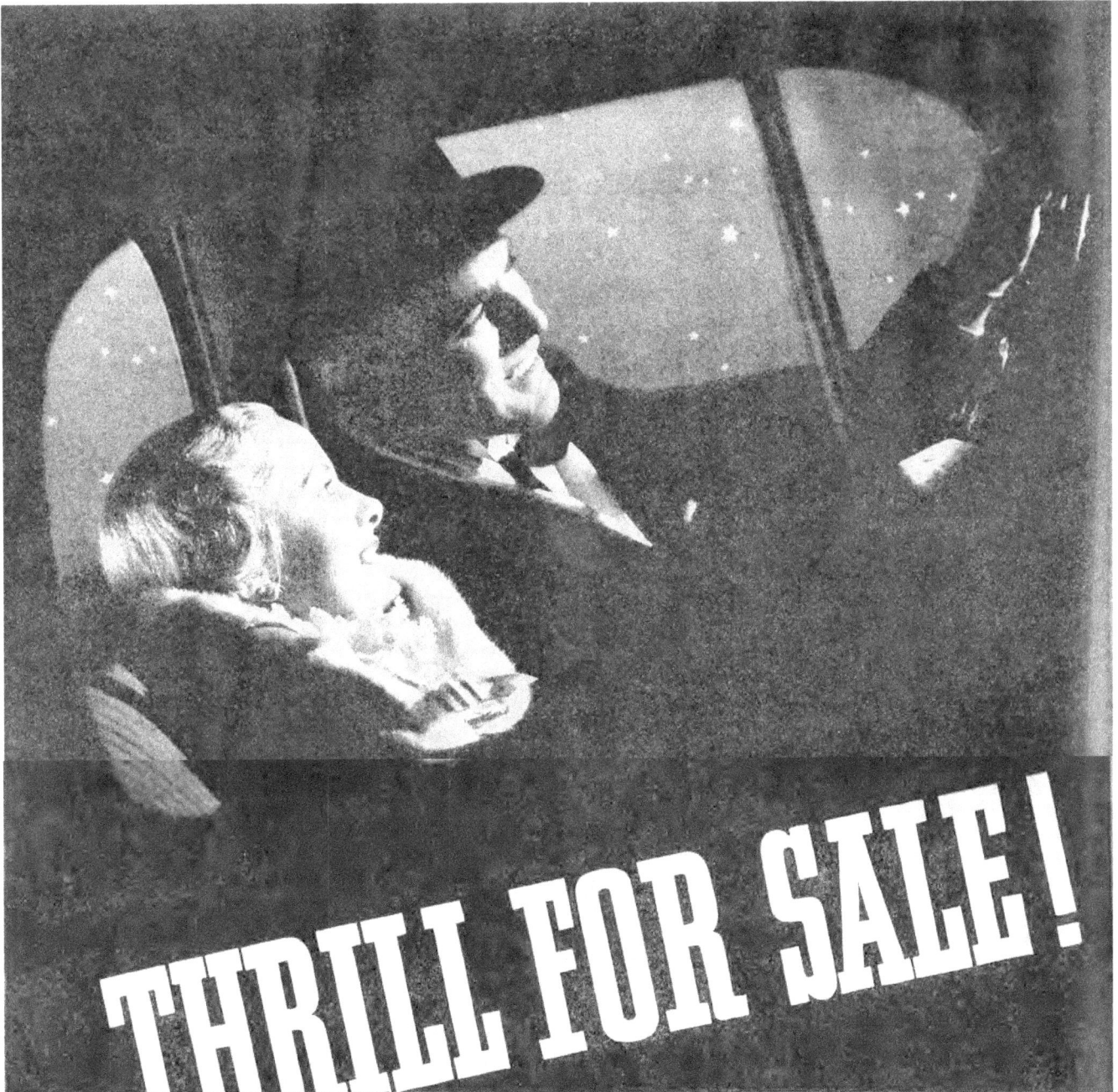

THRILL FOR SALE!

YOU'LL think the driver's seat of that new Buick was tailored to your measure, so comfortably will you settle into place.

You'll think engine-power so silent must be pretty well under wraps, until you give it a shot of gas.

Then things happen. The take-off is instant-fast. There's no laboring pause, no shiver, just that silk-smooth swing into speed.

You head into the open straightaway. Easy, there. Better keep an eye on that speed-ometer needle, you're traveling faster by plenty m.p.h. than you realize.

There's no tension. No strain. There's no threat of that rubbery jumpiness under you

that in many cars keeps you taut and on the alert.

No, this phenomenal performer seems to settle closer and steadier on the road as you press the treadle, and the lightest tip-toe-pressure on those big hydraulics slows you to a safe swerveless stop.

Thrill? Of course! But never the thrill of hazard. The thrill, rather, of beautifully poised mechanism doing whatever you want done without effort or strain.

Better come see this brilliant new Buick, give it a drive, and sample that thrill for yourself.

YOU CAN AFFORD THE NEW BUICK

$765

to $1945 are the list prices at Flint, Mich., subject to change without notice. Standard and special accessories groups on all models at extra cost. All Buick prices include safety glass throughout as standard equipment. Convenient GMAC time payment plan

Buick 8

FIRST OF THE GENERAL MOTORS CARS

Always Simoniz a New Car!

PROTECTS THE FINISH...
MAKES IT LAST LONGER!

SIMONIZING—EASIER
—QUICKER—SAFER

If your car is dull, you can quickly make it look new again with the wonderful Simoniz Kleener. Then apply Simoniz for lasting beauty and protection. ALWAYS INSIST ON THEM FOR YOUR CAR.

The first thing to do for any new car is to Simoniz it! Simoniz is something the finish needs and must have to stay beautiful. It's more than a wax or a polish. In fact, there's nothing like Simoniz! It gives protection to the finish that weather can't wear off. Makes it last longer and keeps the colors from fading. So give your car this world-famous "beauty insurance" that is saving millions time and money. And do it now!

MOTORISTS WISE
SIMONIZ
THE SECRET OF LASTING MOTOR CAR BEAUTY

Simoniz car polish

Performance

PERFORMANCE PROVES THAT FIRESTONE HIGH SPEED TIRES ARE BLOWOUT-PROOF AND GIVE YOU GREATEST TRACTION AND PROTECTION AGAINST SKIDDING

DURING fall and winter months pavements are often slippery with rain, ice and snow and it is important that you have the safest tires you can buy. Tests by a leading university show that Firestone High Speed Tires will stop a car from 15% to 25% quicker than other well known makes.

Gum-Dipping makes the cord body more flexible, tougher and stronger. Leading race drivers, who know tires, will not risk their lives on any other make.

Few car owners fully realize the danger in driving on unsafe tires at today's high speeds. Last year 43,000 accidents were caused by blowouts, punctures and skidding. Don't take chances! Equip your car with Firestone High Speed Gum-Dipped Tires—*the safest tires ever built*—and specify them for your new car.

Your nearby Firestone Auto Supply and Service Store or Firestone Tire Dealer is ready to serve you.

Listen to the Voice of Firestone featuring Richard Crooks, Nelson Eddy, Margaret Speaks, Monday evening over Nationwide N. B. C. — WEAF Network

Firestone

Every one of the winning cars at Indianapolis was equipped with Firestone Gum-Dipped Tires. Not one had a blowout or tire trouble of any kind

For eight years Firestone Gum-Dipped Tires have been on the winning car in the Pike's Peak Climb where a skid means death

Scientific recording instrument used by leading university shows Firestone High Speed Gum-Dipped Tires stop a car 15% to 25% quicker than other well-known makes

On Firestone Gum-Dipped Tires, Ab Jenkins drove 3,000 miles at 127.2 miles per hour, over the hot salt beds of Utah, without a blowout or tire trouble of any kind

The
MASTERPIECE
OF TIRE
CONSTRUCTION

Firestone tires

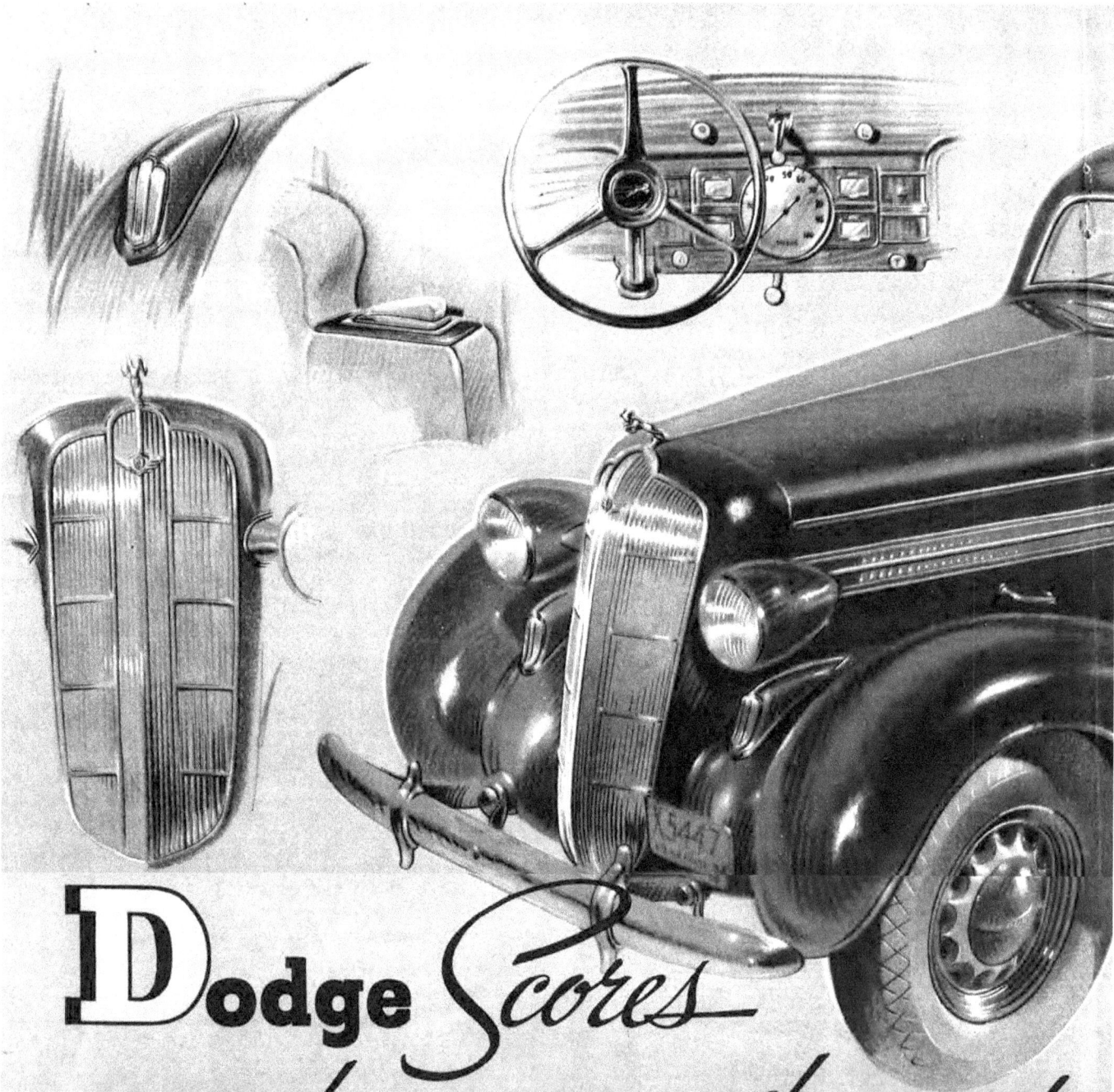

Dodge Scores
another scoop with sensation

FAMOUS for safety, sturdiness, dependability and amazing economy of operation, now the new Dodge for 1936 tops it all by sensationally scoring with breath-taking beauty . . . beauty so startling that it has excited the admiration of everyone who has seen it.

"The smartest and best looking car Dodge ever built," one noted newspaper automobile editor says . . . "A honey!" exclaims another . . . "The most strikingly beautiful of all Dodge cars," writes a third . . . "An eyeful!" is the vote of automobile editors from all parts of the country. "It's easy to see why they call it the 'Beauty Winner'

of 1936," says a famous woman stylist . . . "Its interior appointments will thrill any woman," declares a well-known fashion expert . . .

And no wonder they all rave . . . these men and women who know. At very first sight you'll recognize the sheer beauty and smartness of this new Dodge. Dodge—the car that thrilled all America by setting new records for gas, oil and upkeep savings; the car that has survived the most terrific and tortuous safety tests ever devised; the car that everybody knows is built to "take it."

This "Beauty Winner" of 1936 gives you all the things you should

AMERICA'S BIG MONEY-SAVING CAR...BUILT TO SURV

Dodge

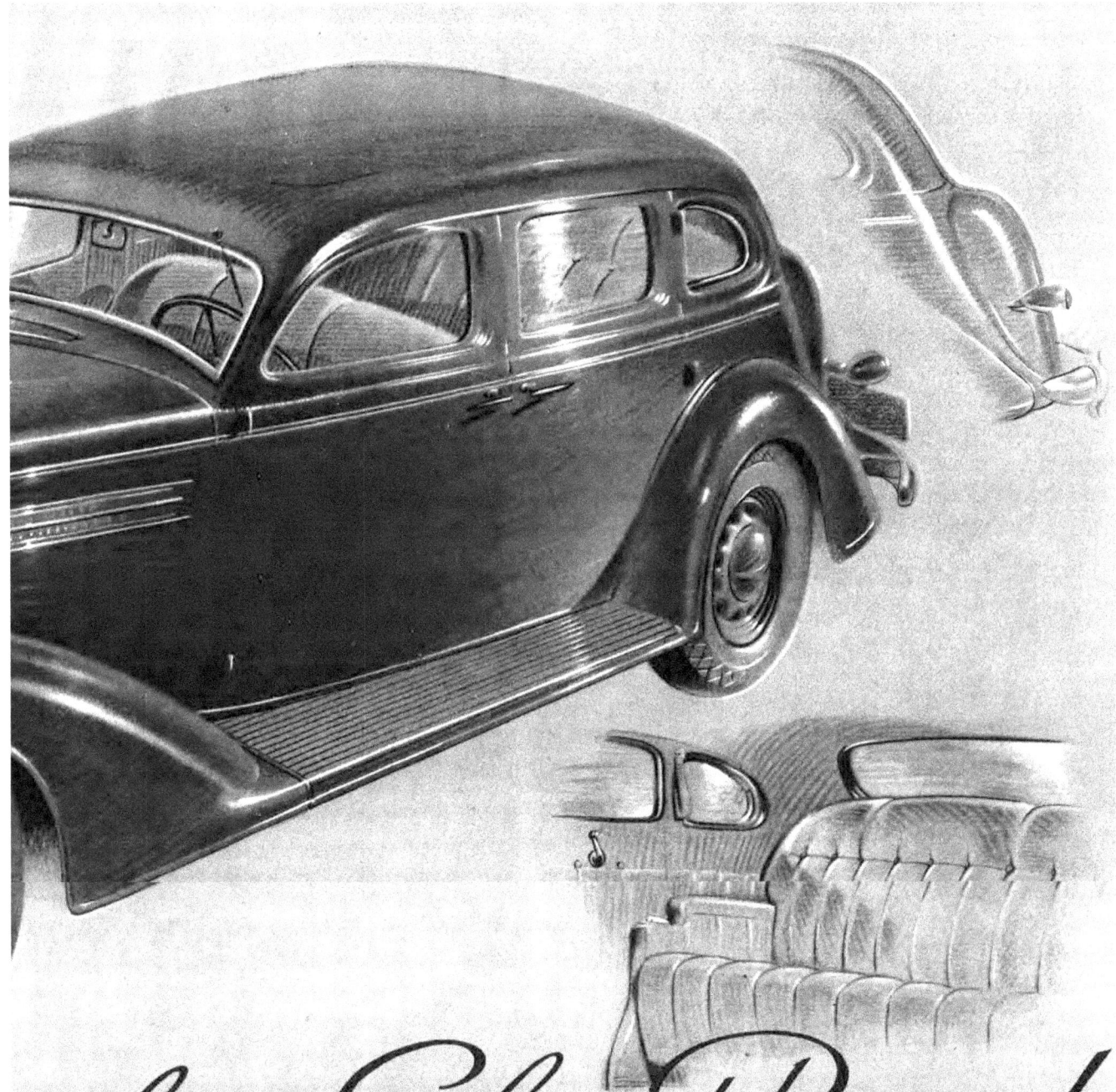

...nal new Style and Beauty!

demand of a motor car—the things you are entitled to. It gives you the kind of ride that would thrill you even in the most expensive American or European motor cars, yet with the amazing economy of operation everyone knows Dodge provides.

It gives you the time-proved safety of *genuine* hydraulic brakes... Dodge safety-steel bodies... the finger-tip, toe-tip handling ease of Balanced Driving Control... new, more spacious interiors, trimmed in richer, more expensive materials... and, above all, it gives you the extraordinary economy of the powerful Dodge engine—the engine which owners are already reporting gives them *18 to 24 miles per gallon of gas and saves up to 20% on oil.*

See this magnificent new Dodge today. Drive it. Compare it point for point with any competitive make priced within $500 of Dodge. You'll be amazed at how much extra value the big Money-Saving "Beauty Winner" of 1936 gives you for just a few dollars more than the lowest-priced cars!

DODGE DIVISION OF CHRYSLER CORPORATION

Time payments to fit your budget. Ask for the official Chrysler Motors Commercial Credit Plan.

...IVE THRILLING SAFETY TESTS.. *Beauty Winner of 1936*

Chrysler Corporation

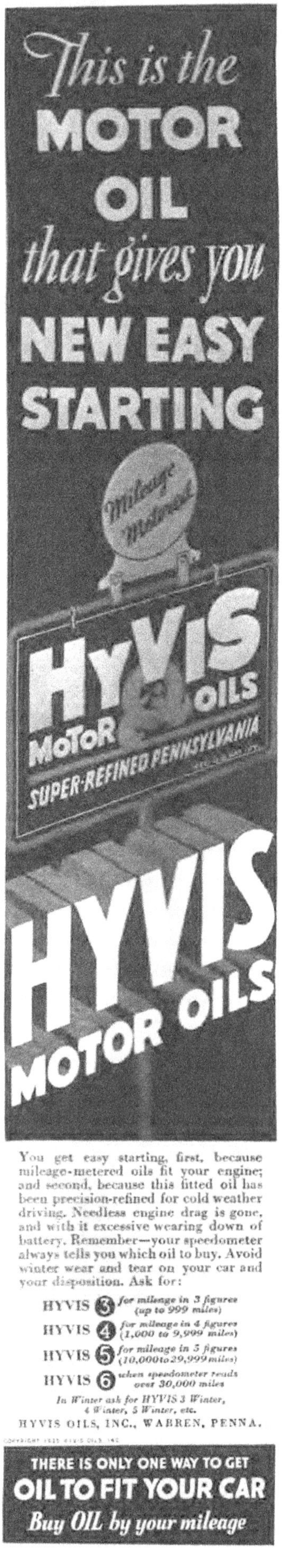

Hyvis Motor Oils

Monday's marketing *can use more gasoline* than Sunday's long trip

Starting, Shifting and Accelerating waste money if your gasoline hasn't these 3 different kinds of Power

4 out of every 5 miles you drive *are stop-and-go*

IT'S the *short* trips . . . to the grocer's, the meat market, the drug store, the bank, the department store . . . that eat up your gasoline!

This is easy to figure out when you consider that one "cold" start can use up a "mile" of gasoline . . . and that rapid accelerating can use 33% more gasoline than just rolling along on a straightaway!

To save money on today's stop-and-go driving, you don't want a gasoline that merely STARTS quickly . . . or one that merely PULLS easily on hills or in shift-ing gears . . . or one that merely gives good MILEAGE on long runs!

You need a gasoline that does ALL THREE of these jobs. In short, you need a BALANCED gasoline!

Shell engineers now offer you the FIRST gasoline of this type . . . the FIRST gasoline made for today's stop-and-go driving.

Stop today at one of the 30,000 neighborly Shell stations from Coast to Coast. Fill up your tank with Super-Shell today and see for yourself how it can save you money.

SAVES in 3 Ways—

STARTING—This *balanced* Super-Shell can save up to a cupful of gaso-line on every "cold" start. Even on sizzling summer days, your engine is relatively "cold" after it has stopped running.

PULLING—It can save up to a cupful in 10 min-utes of rapid accelerating or hill climbing. And you avoid *knocking* which alone in a few minutes can waste up to 10% of your power.

RUNNING—Super-Shell can save up to a cupful of gasoline, motorists report, in an hour on the long stretch—thus saving you money on LONG RUNS as well as on short trips.

Remember, when you save 16 cupfuls, you save a gallon!

Super-SHELL

Saves on today's stop-and-go driving

There are glorious motoring days ahead. Clear, bracing air. Familiar landscapes in Winter dress. Get out and enjoy them. Winter driving is so easy nowadays. Roads cleared. Cars warm and snug. And mechanical worries left behind you *when you use Quaker State Winter Oils and Greases*. These marvelous cold-weather lubricants are the real key to care-free Winter driving. They permit quick starting, and assure safe motor protection when the mercury does a nose-dive.

THIS WINTER-DRIVING LESSON COST H. E. CODY OF ASHTABULA, OHIO, $12.50.   HE OFFERS IT TO YOU FREE

1. "One day last Winter, I let myself be talked into buying a different motor oil... 'just as good as Quaker State' for less money."

2. "Next day it dropped to zero. I had trouble starting because oil had hardened. Drove five miles...wham! Two bearings burned out."

3. "The cost? $12.50 in cash, plus a lot of inconvenience. But it taught me to stick to Quaker State Winter Oil in cold weather."

Look for the Green-and-White Sign and Give Your Car Winter Protection

"First choice of Experience"

QUAKER STATE WINTER OILS AND SUPERFINE WINTER GREASES   •   QUAKER STATE OIL REFINING COMPANY, OIL CITY, PA.

Quaker State Oil

MORE THAN A MILLION
CAR RADIATORS WERE PROTECTED WITH
ZERONE
LAST WINTER!

REG. U.S. PAT. OFF.

THIS WINTER PROTECT YOUR CAR RADIATOR
with the fastest growing anti-freeze in America

A LITTLE more than two years ago du Pont introduced ZERONE to the American motoring public. Last winter more than a million car owners bought it. ZERONE is today the fastest-growing anti-freeze in America.

That's dramatic proof that ZERONE is a good anti-freeze. If ZERONE itself were not so unusually efficient, if ZERONE did not save motorists actual dollars and cents in seasonal protection, then no amount of advertising could have made it, in two short years, the fastest-growing anti-freeze in America.

Try ZERONE this winter; compare its seasonal cost with that of any other anti-freeze you ever used. Follow the simple directions on every can, and discover for yourself, as more than a million car owners already have, that ZERONE offers:

1. An extremely concentrated anti-freeze containing no inactive ingredients.

2. Complete radiator protection against freezing at any temperature.

3. Protection against radiator rust and corrosion.

4. Maximum cooling plant efficiency.

5. Less evaporation — ZERONE is volatile, but is not as evaporative as ordinary low-priced anti-freezes.

6. A conveniently packaged anti-freeze, sealed at the factory in tamper-proof gallon and quart cans for protection against dilution, substitution and adulteration.

7. A development of the du Pont laboratories.

8. Low cost seasonal protection — ZERONE, at $1 a gallon, 25c a quart, is economical to buy and use — comparatively little ZERONE is needed for protection to any temperature.

Today stop at the service station, garage, or accessory store that displays the big blue and yellow ZERONE banner. Get efficient, economical anti-freeze protection this winter . . . E. I. du Pont de Nemours & Co., Inc., ZERONE Sales, Wilmington, Delaware.

$1.00 A GALLON

duPONT
ZERONE
Anti-Rust ANTI-FREEZE

DU PONT ON THE AIR . . . . Listen to "The Cavalcade of America" every Wednesday evening, 8:00 p. m., E. S. T., over CBS coast-to-coast network

Zerone anti-freeze

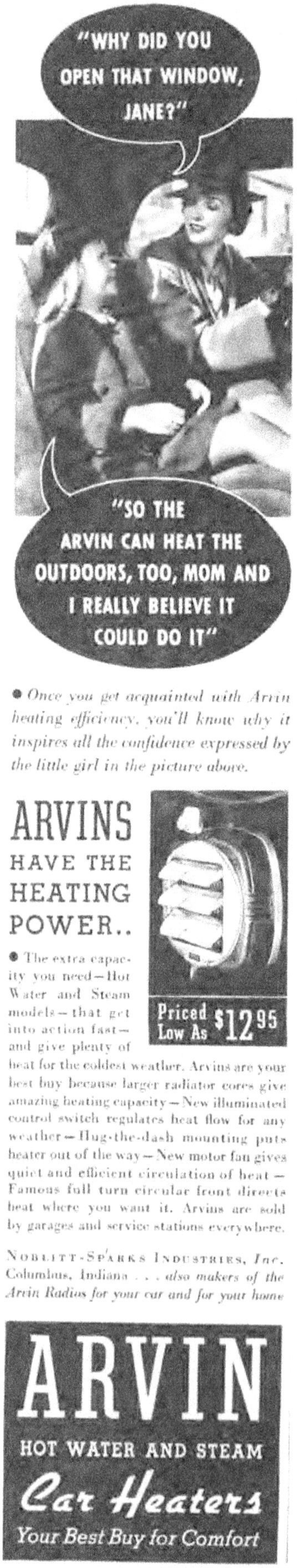

Arvin car heaters

1936 ADS

Don't DRIVE WITH DIRTY OR WORN SPARK PLUGS— *they're costly!*

FOR ECONOMY, SPEND 5c EACH FOR AN AC PLUG CLEANING

Dozens of engineering tests prove that dirty or worn plugs waste as much as one gallon of gas in ten, and cause hard starting and loss of power. With cleaned and adjusted, or new plugs, these same tests show that fuel waste and performance trouble completely disappear.

Millions of thrifty car owners are forming the habit of having their spark plugs cleaned, every 4,000 miles, by a Registered AC Cleaning Station. It's a money-saving habit. It pays for itself, on gas savings alone, in a few hundred miles of driving. And it cures hard starting troubles, and restores full engine power. Why not save gas, yourself—the same way? Get an AC spark plug cleaning today—and save on gas.

LOOK FOR THE SIGN OF "THE PLUG IN THE TUB"

Wherever you see this official sign, there's a Registered AC Spark Plug Cleaning Station. There you will find an expert service man—equipped to render the money-saving AC plug cleaning service—for only 5c a plug—while you wait.

AC SPARK PLUG COMPANY · Flint, Michigan, St. Catharines, Ontario

REPLACE WORN PLUGS AFTER 10,000 MILES with AC QUALITY SPARK PLUGS

—the plugs that have been installed as factory equipment in more than three out of five of the new cars registered in the United States during the past nine years.

AC QUALITY SPARK PLUGS NOW 60c*

*Slightly higher in Canada

AC spark plugs

"Rolling to Fires, I want 100% Hydraulic Brakes!"

SO KNOXVILLE CITY OFFICIALS PICK PLYMOUTH FOR THEIR FIRE CHIEF

C. M. JOHNSON, Chief of Knoxville's efficient Fire Department, likes Plymouth's reliability as well as its safety. "I've got to have a car I can count on," he says.

CITY OFFICIALS of Knoxville, Tenn., gave Fire Chief Johnson his choice of "All Three" leading low-priced cars. He looked them over carefully...compared features and prices...and picked the 1936 Plymouth!

"When an alarm comes in, my car has to roll," he says. "Believe me, I want *double-action* hydraulic brakes on this job...and a Safety-Steel body, too. I've got to have a car I can count on...*all* the time. A big, rugged car that can 'take it' and doesn't tire me

out no matter how many calls I get... day and night. That's why I picked the big 1936 Plymouth!"

Be sure to "Look at All Three" before *you* buy any low-priced car. You will find them priced about alike... but you will also find many extra-value features that give Plymouth a big lead in safety...economy...comfort...reliability...and style. Drive this beautiful new Plymouth! Ask your Chrysler, Dodge or De Soto dealer.

PLYMOUTH DIVISION OF CHRYSLER CORP.

TUNE IN ED WYNN, GRAHAM McNAMEE AND ALL-STAR CAST, TUESDAY NIGHTS, N. B. C. RED NETWORK

(*Above*) FIRE DEPARTMENT SERVICE demands a car that stays out of the repair shop...on the job!

(*Left*) A FIRE CHIEF'S CAR has to travel all kinds of streets. "This Plymouth's riding comfort and handling ease are real blessings," says Chief Johnson.

(*Below*) "I often carry equipment in this big, rear deck space."

EASY TO BUY

Plymouth is priced with the lowest...with terms as low as the lowest! You can buy a Plymouth for $25 a month. The Commercial Credit Co. offers all Chrysler, Dodge and De Soto dealers terms that make Plymouth easy to buy.

$510

AND UP, LIST AT FACTORY, DETROIT SPECIAL EQUIPMENT EXTRA

"PLYMOUTH SAVES MONEY for the city on three counts: on gasoline, oil and upkeep! It's the most economical car we've ever had...and the sturdiest."

PLYMOUTH BUILDS GREAT CARS

An Honest Survey of Car Owners Revealed this :

Mobiloil Lasts Longer...keeps Engines Cleaner...Cuts Repair Bills!

Harry Windle
Brockton, Mass.
CAR OWNER

"I've saved money with Mobiloil since 1916. It's sure a comfort not to have to worry about oil on trips."

J. A. Crain
Evanston, Ill.
AUTO SALESMAN

"You ought to hear how sweet my Ford runs after 10,000 miles using Mobiloil! Never have to add oil between times."

Ludwig Best
Garden City, L. I.
AERO MECHANIC

"Often, I have had to drive beyond an oil change. Mobiloil is the only oil I've found that will stay in my motor."

Mrs. J. Hehn, Jr.
Port Washington, L. I.
HOUSEWIFE

"I no longer spend 60c for 2 quarts of oil with every 10 gallons of gas. I save $4.70 every 1,000 miles with Mobiloil."

W. H. Hanna
Cleveland, Ohio
BOOK STORE PROP.

"Find Mobiloil best of all I tried. Gives us full 1,000 miles in our cars. A big saving, as I drive 35,000 miles a year. Both cars running perfectly."

E. T. Sadler
Chicago, Ill.
ADVERTISING

"In 75,000 miles, I have learned there's a big difference in oils—that Mobiloil is best. I figure it saves me $30 a year."

Start Saving Today with this Oil...See your Mobiloil Dealer

WE ARE PASSING ON TO YOU voluntary reports from 26 users of Mobiloil.

We could explain how Mobiloil is made a *better* oil by the famous Clearosol Process...why it is cleaner, purer, lasts longer, stands up better.

But the real proof is right here...in the *actual savings* reported by people who *watched* costs.

Summer's here...an ideal time to get acquainted with Mobiloil savings. Stop in at the Mobiloil sign or the Sign of the Flying Red Horse. Use the grade recommended by the Official 1936 Mobiloil Chart.

SOCONY-VACUUM OIL COMPANY, INCORPORATED

Lester A. Jeffery
Detroit, Mich.
RADIO TECHNICIAN

"For 8 years I have averaged 1,200 miles to each filling of Mobiloil. No repairs. Wouldn't think of using other kind."

J. R. Jenkins
Albany, N. Y.
HOUSE INSULATOR

"Used Mobiloil exclusively for 10 years. My cars always run fine—no trouble, low oil consumption."

J. McManus
Haverhill, Mass.
BAKERY PRESIDENT

"In changing to Mobiloil, we corrected bearing troubles, bettered mileage... saved 6%, a big item on 42 trucks."

Fred J. Hines
Rochester, N. Y.
GENERAL CONTRACTOR

"We tested many brands of oil on our equipment. Mobiloil proved best...it has cut our oil costs 23%."

T. F. McNaugh
Cleveland, Ohio
TUGBOAT CAPTAIN

"As a user of oil for 35 years, I sure hand the palm to Mobiloil. Makes my car smoother, more powerful."

S. Umina
Cleveland, Ohio
BARBER

"Before changing to Mobiloil, I used to add a quart every 150 miles. Now I can drive 1,000 miles without adding any. I'm saving $25 a year."

G. Whitehurst
Waterford, N. Y.
NURSERY MANAGER

"Long trips, fast driving, don't make any difference to Mobiloil."

F. M. Lansing
Los Angeles, Calif.
MECHANIC

"No matter how old the car, I can always spot the Mobiloil users. Pistons, rings and rods are cleaner, look newer."

Capt. F. Hornke
Roosevelt Field, L. I.
FLYING INSTRUCTOR

"I've used Mobiloil here and in Germany for 20 years. It never forms a gum. Keeps rings tight. Best I've found."

Grace Droney
Boston, Mass.
BEAUTICIAN

"I cover New York, New England, in rain and shine. Mobiloil has cut my oil bill 35%...kept engine free of carbon."

Raymond A. Ely
Rochester, N. Y.
ENGINEER

"I drive my car over 1,500 miles a week. Since switching to Mobiloil, I never have to add a drop between changes."

Mrs. G. Zapf
Rochester, N. Y.
HOUSEWIFE

"I thought all oils were alike, until I used Mobiloil. It goes further."

Joseph Pytko
Wynantskill, N. Y.
GARAGE MANAGER

"Not a bit of engine trouble since I switched to Mobiloil 5 years ago. My motor runs like the day I bought it!"

A. E. Mosier
Kansas City, Mo.
EXECUTIVE

"I have sold and operated machinery of all kinds for 40 years. Never found anything that does Mobiloil's job."

W. H. Monrian
Albany, N. Y.
SALES SUPERVISOR

"25,000 miles a year for 3 years—and never had to add Mobiloil between changes! It drains out looking new."

Joe Bova, Jr.
Cleveland, Ohio
GROCERY STORE PROP.

"Mobiloil has sure delivered extra mileage in our delivery trucks. Always 1,000 miles per crankcaseful."

Don C. Lynn
Montebello, Cal.
TANK LINE OWNER

"In the Imperial Valley, where my trucks run, it hits 120°...hot enough to blister leather! Yet Mobiloil keeps engines cool, saving 30% on oil bills!"

Col. C. P. Dodson
Boston, Mass.
HOTEL MANAGER

"I know hundreds of executives 'on the road.' They concur with me—Mobiloil keeps motors at their top!"

Territ E. Swart
Chicago, Ill.
ACCOUNTANT

"I changed to Mobiloil after just one trial. Sure makes a difference. I no longer have to add quarts."

Robt. H. Glenn
Albany, N. Y.
PHOTOGRAPHER

"3 years on Mobiloil; engine always O. K. Never had a repair due to oil."

Mobiloil

SOCONY-VACUUM Gargoyle Mobiloil

America's Favorite Motor Oil

Mobiloil

YOU'LL BE HAPPIER WITH A *Chrysler*

...AND YOU'LL BE *Money Ahead!*

CHRYSLER puts a thrill in saving money! Gives you the prestige that will make you a proud owner . . . and saves your money with dozens of economy engineering features.

Why drive a gas-eating car . . . when owners of big, handsome Chryslers are reporting 16 to over 20 miles per gallon, as a result of Chrysler's most recent engineering features?

Why spoil your touring fun with a dinky, cramped-up car . . . when Chrysler owners relax in glorious ease while Automatic Overdrive gives them up to 5 extra miles per gallon at touring speeds!

Why not have, in Automatic Overdrive, the newest thrill in motoring . . . when enjoying it means you are saving enough to give you a free mile in every five?

Chrysler's hydraulic brakes are *the pioneer hydraulics* . . . twelve years time-tested. Chrysler pioneered safety-steel bodies . . . naturally, it builds the finest and strongest today.

The difference in paying for a Chrysler and paying for a lowest-priced car figures out as low as ten dollars a month. And the many money-saving features in a fine new Chrysler will cover that difference in mighty short order.

We say you'll be money ahead with a Chrysler . . . any Chrysler dealer will be glad to prove it with clear facts and plain figures.

☆ CHRYSLER SIX . . . 93 horsepower, 118-inch wheelbase, $760 and up.

☆ DE LUXE EIGHT . . . 105 and 110 horsepower, 121 and 133-inch wheelbase, $995 and up.

☆ AIRFLOW EIGHT . . . 115 horsepower, 123-inch wheelbase. All models, $1345.

$760*

☆ AIRFLOW IMPERIAL . . . 130 horsepower, 128-inch wheelbase. All models, $1475.

☆ AIRFLOW CUSTOM IMPERIAL . . . 130 horsepower, 137-inch wheelbase, $2475 and up.

†Automatic Overdrive is standard on Airflow Imperial. Available on all 1936 Chrysler at slight additional cost.

*All prices list at factory, Detroit; special equipment extra.

Ask for the Official Chrysler Motors Commercial Credit Company Time Payment plan Available through all Chrysler Dealers.

MONEY-SAVING MIRACLE... Chrysler's Automatic Overdrive. Cuts engine speed one-third at car speeds over 40. Actually gives you one free mile in every five!

16 TO 20 MILES PER GALLON. Some Chrysler owners report even more! Big savings too in oil consumption. A Chrysler costs less to drive than many smaller cars.

ENGINEERED TO SAVE MONEY! There are savings in Chrysler's time-tested hydraulic brakes . . . safety-steel bodies . . . Floating Power . . . valve seat inserts

LOWER REPAIR BILLS...LONGER LIFE. Chrysler gives you finest quality and top-ranking engineering. It costs less to run . . . needs fewer repairs . . . lasts longer

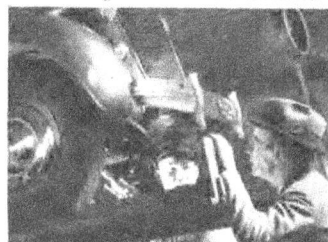

Chrysler Corporation

Want More Miles per Gallon?

Choose the Spark Plugs Champions Use

GUARANTEED DEPENDABLE

CHAMPION PATENTED

CHAMPION EXTRA RANGE SPARK PLUGS

If you had two cars that were precisely alike—except that one was equipped with Champion Spark Plugs and one with some other brand—and you drove each of these cars every other day—you would soon learn a very startling lesson. You would find, as the miles accumulated on the speedometer, that the car equipped with Champions would perform better, give better gasoline mileage, and operate more dependably. That is the reason why Champions are preferred both at home and abroad—and why every important race in the last twelve years has been won with Champions. Insist on Champions especially if you are not already using them.

W. PALM BEACH, FLA.—Champions made a clean sweep of the 29th Washington's Birthday Regatta. Chris Ripp won permanent possession of coveted Royal Poinciana and Col. E. R. Bradley Trophies. Exclusive Sillimanite insulators have made Champions a byword for dependability.

DAYTONA BEACH, FLA.—The recent 250 mile Stock Car Beach and Road Race was won by Milt Marion in a Ford V-8. All cars finishing used Champions. Champion Extra-Range design provided the heat range necessary for full power in deep sand as well as full speed on hard level stretches.

CHICAGO—Keeshin Motor Express Co., Inc., one of the world's foremost motor freight lines operates over 1400 units, traveling 16,000 direct miles daily. Famous for its efficiency, Keeshin uses Champions to meet varying performance requirements and operating conditions.

FRANCE—Etancelin, driving a Champion-equipped Maserati, won the recent Grand Prix Pau. The first four to finish used Champions. The necessity for extreme engine flexibility in European road racing explains the almost universal use of Champions by leading race drivers.

TO RID YOUR CAR OF MOTOR "BUGS" INSTALL A SET OF CHAMPION PLUGS

Champion spark plugs

SEE.. DRIVE.. PRICE THEM ALL ... and

A General Motors Value

YES, you'll come back to Pontiac and here's what will bring you back: *Silver Streak styling* that gains in distinction the more you look about you. *Luxury* that becomes more incredible the more comparisons you make. *Economy* that equals or surpasses that of smaller, lighter cars. (Official record of the Pontiac Six is 23.9 miles per gallon.) A record for *dependability* that is unique in the industry. (83 per cent of all Pontiacs ever built are still in daily use.) *Advancements* that put Pontiac on a plane with the greatest cars ever built. And a first-cost that brings Pontiac so close to the very lowest in price that, as little as $1.00* extra a week, over a year's period, will cover the difference!

There, in 100 words, is a story of value new to the automotive industry. In it you will find the cause of Pontiac's firm hold on its growing public. Owners stand by Pontiac for the very practical reason that they have nothing to gain and much to lose by switching to another car. Find out why—make comparisons—*track down the truth*. Every new fact will point to Pontiac as the logical car to buy.

List prices at Pontiac, Michigan, begin at $615 for the Six and $730 for the Eight (subject to change without notice). Safety glass standard equipment on De Luxe Six and Eight. Monthly payments to suit your purse on the General Motors Installment Plan. Standard group of accessories extra. ★Lowest priced Pontiac Coupe versus the average of the de luxe coupe prices of three leading low-priced cars. Based on delivered prices in a centrally located metropolis.

YOU'LL COME BACK TO PONTIAC!

THE MOST BEAUTIFUL THING ON WHEELS

PONTIAC $615*
THE BIG ECONOMY *Six*

America's Cars Make ¾ Billion STOPS a Day!

ST. LOUIS, MO.—12th and Market! 70 cars stop every minute between 5 and 6 P.M. Many cars average 5 shifts in two blocks, even though the two intersecting streets are very broad.

TROY, N.Y.—Driving 7 blocks in the business district, from Congress and 3rd Streets to Jacob and River Streets, a reporter had to stop 10 times. In this short distance, he had to shift 30 times.

NEW ORLEANS, LA.—A test car took 6 minutes to drive 9 blocks down Canal Street. It had to make 7 stops. An average of 20,531 cars pass the busy corner of Canal and Rampart Streets every day.

4 out of every 5 miles you drive are "STOP-and-GO"

EACH DAY America's 25 million cars average 30 stops... making ¾ of a billion in all. Each stop eats up gasoline... in starting, shifting, accelerating!

Accelerating alone, leading auto engineers say, can use up 60% more gasoline than steady running.

For economy in "stop-and-go" driving, your gasoline needs 3 kinds of power—just as your car needs 3 different shifts of gears. You need one kind of power for *quick starts*, one for *fast pickup* and hill climbing, and still another for *steady running*.

Super-Shell combines these 3 different kinds of power in one fuel—THE FIRST TRULY BALANCED GASOLINE.

Super-Shell is on sale at more than 30,000 neighborly Shell stations from coast to coast.

PASADENA, CAL.—An investigator drove 10 blocks through the busiest part of town. Over *half* of his time was spent standing still. His average speed was only 9 miles an hour, although he tried to see how fast he could travel the distance. Over *one-fifth* of the time, the car was in low gear.

SUPER ⬡ SHELL

Shell gasoline

FORD V·8 TRUCK DOES 68,000 MILES WITHOUT TAKING HEAD OFF ENGINE

Some of the Ford V-8 Trucks operated by the Great Southern Trucking Company have run as high as 68,000 miles with heavy loads. Yet it hasn't even been necessary to remove the engine-heads. Repair costs have been cut to the minimum.

Ford V-8 Trucks fit right into the for-hire hauling business. They get over the roads on faster schedules, and give customers better competitive service. They can carry the extra tons that spell more profit for the operator, without the cost per mile running into extra expense that whittles down earnings.

The Great Southern Trucking Company fleet is meeting every one of these exacting specifications. Fixed costs are less . . . licenses, taxes, depreciation, etc. On the main highways of America, Ford fleets are proving that they can handle any kind of a truck job—at minimum cost per mile.

You can test the Ford V-8 Truck with your own loads before you actually lay down the money for it. Your Ford dealer will gladly lend you his own demonstrator truck or commercial car. Try it. See how it handles your jobs. It won't cost you a penny. It may save you many dollars.

One of the new 131½-inch chassis with closed cab now being used profitably by the Great Southern Trucking Company.

THE ONLY TRUCK THAT GIVES YOU A V-8 ENGINE... PLUS THESE ADDITIONAL FEATURES

Full-floating rear axle with straddle-mounted pinion . . . full torque-tube and radius-rod drive . . . quick-action safety brakes . . . big, 11-inch heavy-duty clutch . . . truck-type four-speed transmission . . . deep, rugged frame with full-channel-depth cross-members . . . durable baked-enamel finish.

● Any new 112-inch wheelbase Ford V-8 Commercial Car can be purchased for $25 a month, with usual down-payment. Any new 131½-inch or 157-inch wheelbase Ford V-8 Truck can be purchased with the usual down-payment on the new UCC ½% per month Finance Plans.

Ford V·8 Trucks
AND COMMERCIAL CARS

Ford V-8 trucks

Quality-built...
for Real Economy

...low operating cost, low maintenance cost and year-after-year dependability

POWERFUL, ECONOMICAL ENGINE

SOLID-STEEL "TURRET-TOP" BODY

POWERFUL, ECONOMICAL ENGINE—Proving ground tests and the records of owners establish that Oldsmobile's month-in-month-out gasoline and oil consumption is extraordinarily low ... while its power is more than ample to meet the hardest driving demands.

SOLID-STEEL "TURRET-TOP" BODIES BY FISHER—To the protection of steel over head, steel under foot and steel all around, Oldsmobile adds the security of Safety Glass throughout at no extra cost. No Draft Ventilation admits fresh air without drafts.

KNEE-ACTION WHEELS AND CENTER-CONTROL STEERING—Oldsmobile's independently sprung front wheels "step over" bumps and holes—provide a restful, gliding ride. They also permit the use of Center-Control Steering—easy, shock-proof and true.

SUPER-HYDRAULIC BRAKES and BIG, LOW-PRESSURE TIRES—The extra-large braking area of Oldsmobile's powerful, Super-Hydraulic Brakes combines with the traction of Oldsmobile's big, low-pressure tires to assure quick, smooth, straight-line stops.

RUGGED KNEE-ACTION WHEELS

BIG SUPER-HYDRAULIC BRAKES

MONTHLY PAYMENTS TO SUIT YOUR PURSE!

Compare Oldsmobile's low delivered prices and the new, greatly reduced General Motors Instalment Plan — the lowest financing cost in the history of the General Motors Acceptance Corporation — a decided advantage to those who buy on time.

GENERAL MOTORS INSTALMENT PLAN

New Low Prices
$665

SIXES $665 and up, EIGHTS $810 and up
list prices at Lansing, subject to change without notice. Safety Glass standard equipment all around. Special accessory groups extra. The car illustrated is the Six-Cylinder Touring Sedan, $860. In
A GENERAL MOTORS VALUE

OLDSMOBILE is a thoroughly economical car —economical in the complete and *genuine* sense. *Real* economy, as experienced motorists know, is not a matter of "miles per gallon" alone. *Real* economy is a combination of low fuel and oil costs, low maintenance expense and low depreciation. Measured by this practical yardstick, Oldsmobile is the wisest investment for anyone's motoring dollar. Oldsmobile offers the advanced engineering that means low operating and upkeep costs—the quality materials and workmanship that mean long life and high resale value. But Oldsmobile goes further still. At its definitely low price, and with all its real economy, Oldsmobile provides every modern, fine-car feature—everything for smooth, lively performance—everything for utmost comfort, driving ease and safety. Take a trial drive in Oldsmobile and judge for yourself!

OLDSMOBILE 6 & 8
"The Car that has Everything"

Invitations to You

...AND A NEW TOURING SERVICE THAT MAKES IT EASY TO ACCEPT THEM ALL!

Which of the 48 States have you never visited? This summer there's something new, something exciting to enjoy in them all.

This summer, too, you can see America at its best. A new and enlarged Texaco Touring Service . . . the most complete service of its kind ever developed . . . stands ready to help you plan your trips and route them, *without cost to you!*

This nation-wide organization with seven convenient bureaus throughout America will insure your freedom from road discomforts.

With the assistance of thousands of cooperating dealers in the 48 States, Texaco Touring Service provides you with maps . . . marks your best route . . . plans your trip to take advantage of up-to-the-minute information regarding road conditions.

En route, the service of Texaco dealers is available wherever you drive . . . at stations where you will receive the same thoughtful service, the same emergency-grade Fire-Chief gasoline you get at home.

Read below how this unique touring service works for you. Choose your trip. Then see your nearest Texaco dealer for quick travel help . . . or use the convenient coupon now.

HOW YOUR TOURING SERVICE REQUESTS ARE ATTENDED TO

You RECEIVE

YOU AVOID
BAD ROADS
UNCERTAINTY
DETOURS

TEXACO TOURING SERVICE
Address Branch Office nearest to you

1400 Boardwalk, Atlantic City, N. J.
332 S. Michigan Ave., Chicago, Ill.   929 So. B'dway, Los Angeles, Cal.
210 Fourteenth St., Denver, Colo.   200 S. Miami Ave., Miami, Fla.
720 San Jacinto, Houston, Tex.   135 E. 42nd St., New York, N. Y.

Please send me a trip to _____
To _____
via _____
I plan to start about _____
Name _____
Address _____

TEXACO TOURING SERVICE

A free service by the makers of ***FIRE-CHIEF*** *—used by more tourists than any other gasoline*

Texaco Touring Service

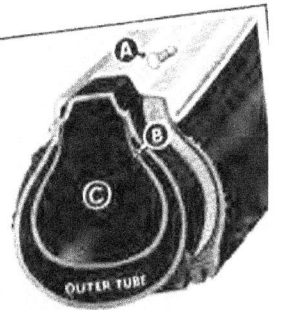

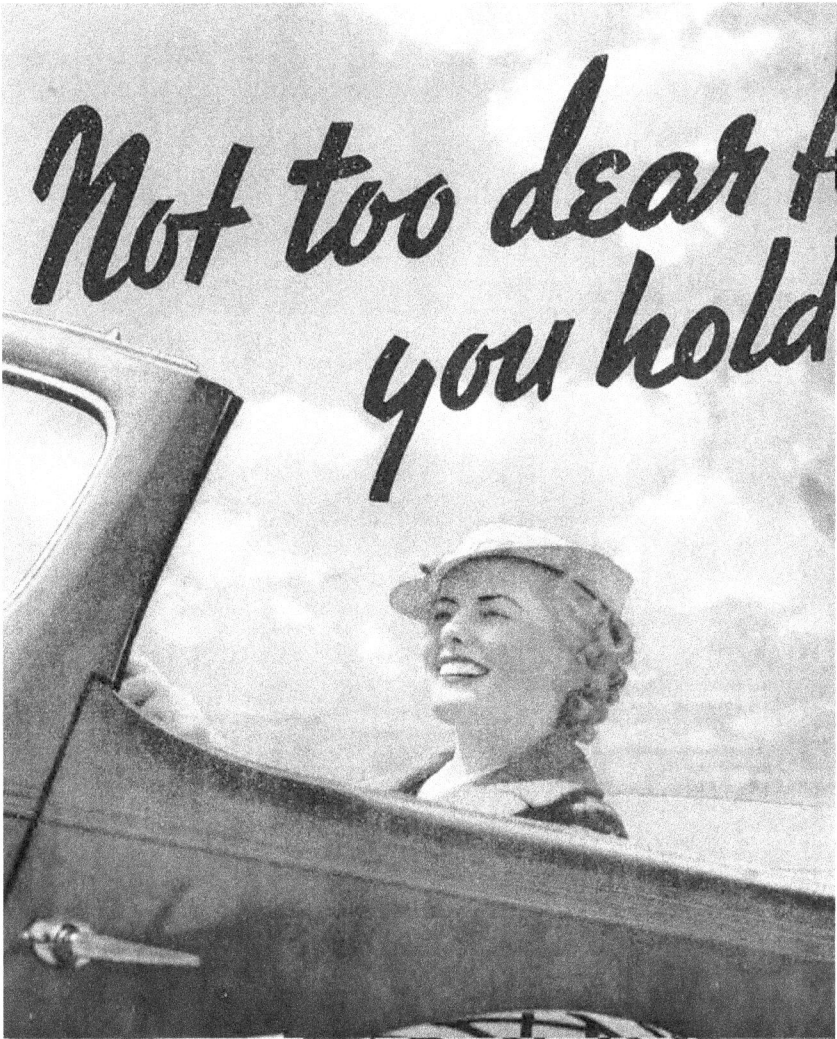

Goodyear Tires

Chicago's Merchandise Mart, world's largest building, has 9,031 windows and doors to clean

LIFE'S AT STAKE

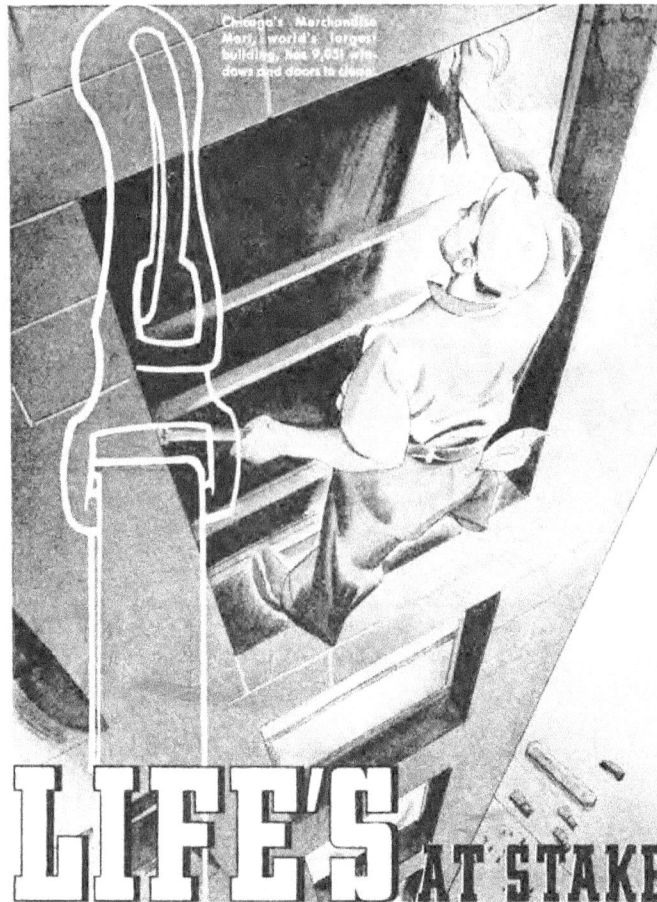

You can trust NEW PENNZOIL to protect your motor...like the window washer trusts his safety belt, far above the street

● Put new Pennzoil in your crank-case and you can safely forget it for miles and miles of hard going. Its extra-tough film gives you adequate protection against extremes of heat, friction and pressure . . . and it *lasts longer*.

New Pennzoil saves you money in three important ways.

Smoother operation gives you more miles per gallon of gas. Pennzoil's exceptional film stands up longer...giving more miles between oil changes...less "adding

a quart"...actually saving up to 50% on oil costs. And there's no sludge to gum up valves and piston rings, wasting power and causing big repair bills.

Millions of car owners, leading air lines, new streamline trains and prize-winning race drivers...all know that only Pennzoil can do a Pennzoil lubrication job. It's *safest* for your car.

Go to your independent Pennzoil dealer for a *complete* lubrication service.

Member Penn. Grade Crude Oil Assn. Permit No. 2

United Air Lines uses Pennzoil in the world's largest fleet of high speed transport planes.

BONDED PENNZOIL DEALER
100% Pure Pennsylvania
PENNZOIL
Safe Lubrication

MORE MILES OF SAFE LUBRICATION

Pennzoil

LIGHT for the LAW!

"Calling all cars—calling all cars" . . . the radio drones on and on, as "the law" speeds to the scene of trouble. Delco-Remy has been a leader in the field of extra-capacity generator equipment demanded by the short-wave radio, searchlights, and other accessories of the modern police cruiser. From its experience in police installations has come other generator equipment of extra capacity for passenger cars and commercial vehicles, so that you, too, may have the dependable operation of your own car's radio, spotlights, heater, cigar lighter, and other motoring conveniences. When you think of anything electrical on your car, think of Delco-Remy.

*

Extra-capacity generators with forced-draft ventilation, current and voltage regulators, and powerful, rugged Delco batteries are available for vehicles where extra current is needed. Delco-Remy has available the proper generator and battery to provide dependable starting, lighting, and ignition for your needs.

Delco-Remy

MANUFACTURERS OF DELCO-REMY STARTING, LIGHTING, AND IGNITION • KLAXON HORNS • DELCO BATTERIES • AUTOMATIC CARBURETOR CONTROLS

UNITED SERVICE MOTORS

DELCO-REMY PRODUCTS AND GENUINE PARTS ARE AVAILABLE AT CONVENIENT UNITED MOTORS SERVICE STATIONS EVERYWHERE . . . WHEREVER YOU SEE THIS SIGN.

DelcoRemy batteries

Just look at

More headroom than in all but one or two of the most expensive cars!

Greater comfort . . . greater safety . . . better ventilation . . . when there's more than enough room over your head for a top hat!

Relax, stretch out and ride in luxurious comfort!

In Nash "400" or LaFayette you ride in a comfortable, natural position— cradled between the two axles

Wider seats than in cars costing over $2,000!

Three big people—even six-footers—ride in front or back seat with room to spare! What a relief—if you've been cooped up in a small car!

Car shown is Nash "400" De Luxe four-door sedan with trunk

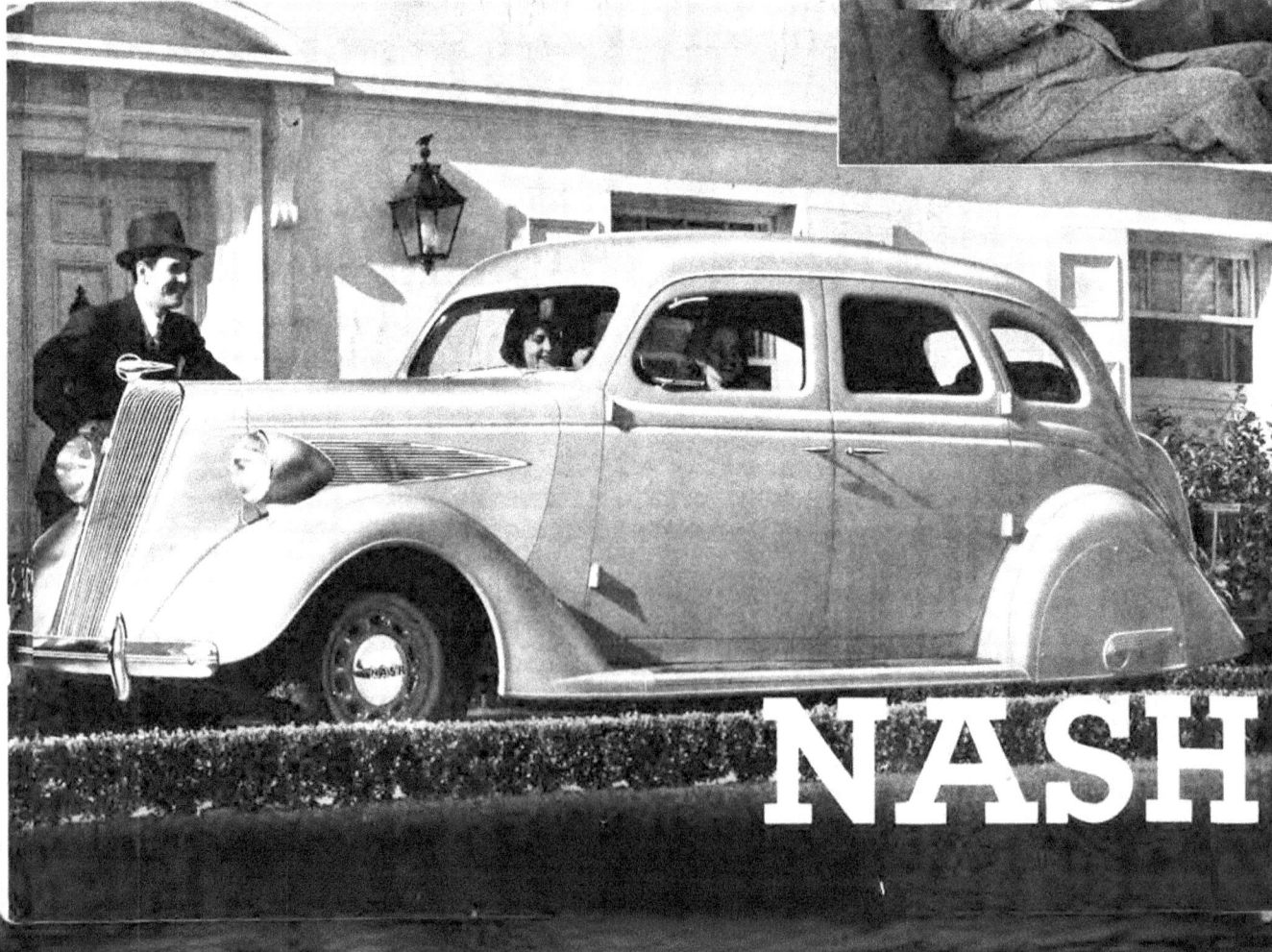

NASH

Nash 400

the difference!

NASH "400" AND LaFAYETTE GIVE YOU

more room

THAN IN CARS COSTING TWO AND THREE TIMES AS MUCH

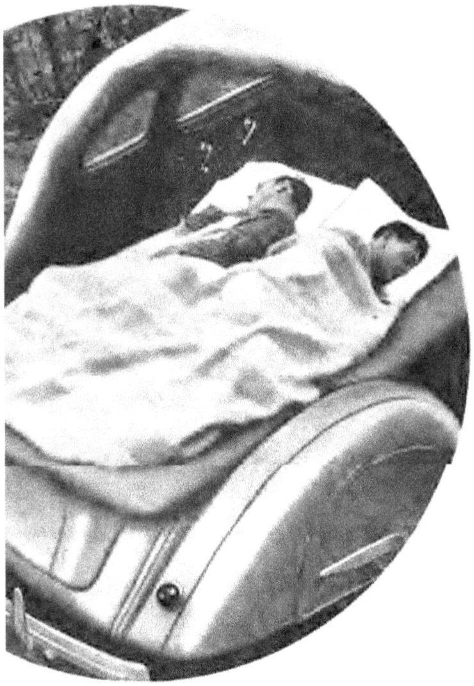

Enough Room to make a 6-foot double bed without using the front seat space!

Arranged inside any Nash "400" or LaFayette sedan—in less than 10 minutes. Great for camping, touring. No mattress or extra equipment needed. Cuts travel costs!

Other low-priced cars MAY offer you this much room NEXT year or in the future—but you get it in Nash "400" and LaFayette NOW!

Why ride cramped and cooped up in a small car when you can enjoy the luxury of roominess? Nash "400" and LaFayette offer you MUCH MORE ROOM than any other car in the low-priced fields . . . in fact, more room than you can get in all but a few of the more expensive cars!

Wider seats than in cars costing over $2,000! More headroom than you'll find in cars costing hundreds, even thousands, of dollars more! More legroom, too. You ride in luxurious comfort, cradled between the two axles—not over them.

But extra roominess is only one of the high-priced-car features that you get in Nash "400" and LaFayette. They give you the world's first complete seamless all-steel body . . . the largest, double-acting hydraulic brakes in relation to car weight ever put on any car at any price! They're lower, too, and wider than other low-priced cars! And they give you all of the vital features of engineering that other manufacturers LEAVE OUT of their low-priced cars!

Automatic Cruising Gear!

Nash "400" and LaFayette are the only cars in the low-priced fields that offer you, at slight extra cost, the sensational gas-saving Automatic Cruising Gear. This automatic "fourth gear" reduces engine revolutions ¼ at high speeds, minimizes wear on moving parts, saves up to 25% in gasoline, up to 50% on oil! The Nash Motors Company, Kenosha, Wisconsin.

SPECIAL TOURING FEATURES!

Cut travel costs . . . give more miles per dollar . . . increase vacation pleasure! • ***Sleeping Car*** — Any Nash "400" or LaFayette sedan instantly converted into a six-foot bed with seat cushions. • ***Large Luggage Compartment*** — in every model. • ***Automatic Cruising Gear*** — gives 4 to 5 more miles per gallon on cross-country driving. • Ask for a Touring Demonstration.

Look how LaFayette—the lowest-priced Nash-built car—compares with cars in and above its price class. All other Nash cars are as large or larger in every dimension!

CAR	WIDTH OF SEAT Front	WIDTH OF SEAT Back	HEADROOM Front	HEADROOM Back	LEGROOM Front	LEGROOM Back
LaFayette	52½	49	38	38	20	25
Car A	46	45¼	37½	37¾	18½	24
Car B	50½	47	37¼	36½	18	18¾
Car C	47½	45½	37¼	36½	19½	20¼
Car D	51¼	46	37¼	35½	18¾	21¼
Car E	49½	45¾	36¼	36⅛	19	20½
Car F	50¾	45¼	35¾	35¼	19½	20⅝
Car G	51½	45¾	36	35½	18¾	19¾
A $2,000 car	50	49	34½	36	20	24
A $3,000 car	51	49	38	38	20	25

NASH "400" **$665** AND UP F. O. B. FACTORY LaFAYETTE **$595** AND UP F. O. B. FACTORY

and LaFAYETTE

Big, luxurious Nash Ambassador sedans with trunks—125-inch wheelbase—only $835 to $995 at the factory. Special equipment extra. All prices are subject to change without notice. • CONVENIENT, LOW MONTHLY PAYMENTS THROUGH NEW 6% C.I.T. BUDGET PLAN

Nash LaFayette

The Same
Strength of Character
in Big Six-Wheeler
and Light-Delivery
International Trucks

Many of the toughest hauling assignments in the world fall to *International* Six-Wheel Trucks. The contractor knows from experience that he can count on Internationals for power, stamina, and economy. He knows that International service will keep them on the job. Whatever his work—from building a dam to mastering the remotest oilfield —he feels *safe* with Internationals.

You are in a special class if you use trucks like these, but no matter what your hauling requirements, *any* International will give you *heavy-duty stamina in proportion.* There is *extra* all-truck value in all the 28 International models, down to the Half-Ton chassis priced at $400 f. o. b. factory.

Write for the 32-page catalog on the International Six-Wheelers—the Half-Ton folder—or information on any intermediate size. The nearest Company-owned branch or International dealer is at your service.

INTERNATIONAL HARVESTER COMPANY
606 S. Michigan Ave.   (INCORPORATED)   Chicago, Illinois

Illustration: International Dual-Drive Six-Wheel Truck, Model C-55-F, maximum carrying capacity 23,000 lbs. International Six-Wheelers, Dual-Drive and Trailing-Axle, range from 11,400 lbs. up. Wheelbase lengths 168 to 244 in., permitting bodies for a wide variety of application.

INTERNATIONAL

INTERNATIONAL TRUCKS

"Oklahoma's Oil Fields are My Office"

"MY DESK IS AT THE WHEEL OF THIS 1936 PLYMOUTH"

**CERTIFIED INTERVIEW WITH
F. D. CUMMINGS, DISTRICT PROD. SUPT.,
SKELLY OIL CO., INC., TULSA, OKLA.**

FOR 40 YEARS, F. D. Cummings has been getting gas and oil out of the ground. Now a big 1936 Plymouth helps him superintend production at 140 Skelly oil wells.

"The company told me to select a car," says Mr. Cummings, "and I picked Plymouth. I drive about 3,000 miles a month through these oil fields ... and Plymouth's comfort and ease of handling are real blessings.

"Hydraulic brakes and a Safety-Steel body made it easy to choose Plymouth. I've never had an accident ... and don't intend to."

Mr. Cummings praises Plymouth's engineering. "No wonder it's so economical to run!"

You may not do one-third the driving Mr. Cummings does. But you *do* want the safety, comfort, economy and reliability that made him choose a Plymouth.

Get out on the road with a new Plymouth ... that will tell you the story. Just ask your Chrysler, Dodge or De Soto dealer.

PLYMOUTH DIVISION OF CHRYSLER CORP.

EASY TO BUY

"Plymouth is priced with the lowest ... and Plymouth terms are as low as the lowest! You can buy a big, new Plymouth for as little as $25 a month with usual down payment ... The Commercial Credit Company has made available to all Chrysler, Dodge and De Soto Dealers low finance terms that make Plymouth easy to buy."

$510

AND UP, LIST AT FACTORY, DETROIT — SPECIAL EQUIPMENT EXTRA

"THERE'S NO VIBRATION ... with Floating Power ... in a Plymouth."

"IT'S REMARKABLE how easy this Plymouth is on gas, oil and upkeep."

MR. CUMMINGS contrived a pulley for the rear wheel of his Plymouth, as picture shows ... which reels in the piano-wire line used to plumb oil well depth (several thousand feet).

(*Left*) "THIS OIL FIELD COUNTRY certainly makes the man behind the wheel thankful for Plymouth's power, stamina and comfort," Mr. Cummings says. "Plymouth sure stands up!"

AT ONE OF THE 140 WELLS of which Mr. Cummings is production superintendent ... with the company-owned 1936 Plymouth he selected. "I always feel safe in Plymouth," he says. "I'm glad its body is Safety-Steel ... and the brakes 100% Hydraulic!"

PLYMOUTH BUILDS GREAT CARS

Plymouth

THE helpless are no longer helpless against the risk and peril of blowouts—not if you put Goodyear Double Eagle Airwheels* and LifeGuard* tubes on your family car. Built to stand with sleepless vigilance between your passengers and any tire hazard, this combination is the finest safety equipment now purchasable in the world. Nothing has been spared to make these twin Goodyear guardians trustworthy beyond any fault or flaw—their mission being not to save money, but to save life.

EIGHT STANDOUT FEATURES

which lift the new Double Eagle Airwheel above any tire we have ever built*

1 The finest, safest, handsomest, longest mileage tire that we have ever built.

2 The best-proved non-skid tread pattern in the world, made more efficient.

3 Tougher rubber in this tread, slotted 15% deeper to give longer non-skid life than even the famed Goodyear "G-3."

4 Built throughout of special new heat fighting compound that frees high speed travel from tread-throwing risk.

5 Extra rubber "float" for every ply, new "rubber-rivet" breaker-strip anchorage, stronger bead.

6 Supertwist cord in every ply to guard against bruises, fatigue, shoulder breaks.

7 Flexible, easy-rolling casing without the tread stiffness common to heavy tires.

8 Built to strictest specifications in industry, in materials, workmanship, balance and inspection.

MORE PEOPLE RIDE ON GOODYEAR TIRES THAN ON ANY OTHER KIND

★ Trade-mark Reg. U.S. Pat. Off.

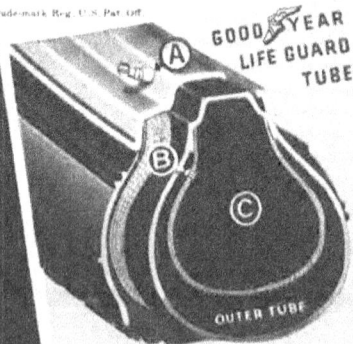

GOODYEAR LIFE GUARD TUBE

OUTER TUBE

A Look for the yellow valve stem and blue cap

B LifeGuards* take a little longer to inflate because air passes gradually from "inner tire" to outer tube through this VENT HOLE

C On this two-ply "INNER TIRE" you ride to a stop with car under control, even though casing and outer tube blow wide open

Goodyear Tires

This strange FACT!

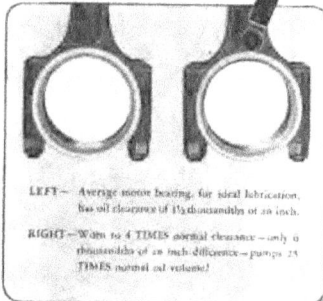

LEFT— Average motor bearing, for ideal lubrication, has oil clearance of 1½ thousandths of an inch.

RIGHT— Worn to 4 TIMES normal clearance — only a thousandths of an inch difference — pumps 25 TIMES normal oil volume!

proves that WORN BEARINGS cause OIL PUMPING

NO WONDER then that *partial* overhaul, such as new rings, does not restore power, pep, performance. It is unreasonable to expect it—when the trouble starts at worn connecting rod and main bearings! For example, an average bearing worn 2 times normal clearance actually pumps 5 TIMES more oil. Worn 4 times normal, it pumps 25 TIMES more oil. *Just a few thousandths of an inch difference between fine, snappy, economical performance and a slow, sluggish oil hog!* New rings can't handle such excessive oil pumping, because they are soon caked and plugged with carbon, and useless for oil control.

WHEN YOUR CAR USES TOO MUCH OIL, BE SURE TO CHECK THE BEARINGS!

When the motor is opened for new rings, pistons or cylinder reboring, which all do their part, tell your service man to check the main and connecting rod bearings. If worn, replace with Federal-Mogul bearings. They are engineered for the job of oil control. And you get a COMPLETE job done, where every part can perform at its best and most economically.

For 38 years Federal-Mogul has been a leading producer of precision-made bearings and bushings for the automotive industry.

FEDERAL-MOGUL CORPORATION
DETROIT, MICHIGAN

REPLACE WITH

Mogul FEDERAL

"We've never owned a NEW car

but...we know how to get

NEW CAR PERFORMANCE with SEALED POWER PISTON RINGS"

"Why, SURE! We'd like to own a shiny 1936 model. But the budget says 'no!' So we grin, pile into the car, give 'er the gas, and go!... Our car had 30,000 on the speedometer when we bought it—but it was the best we could afford. Lazy at lights, a laggard on hills, not very fast anywhere—it gave 11 miles to the gallon on good days, and we 'put in a quart of oil' every time we filled the gas tank. Then a Sealed Power Repairman told us about Sealed Power Sta-Tite Piston Rings, engineered especially for WORN motors by one of the oldest and largest of makers of rings for NEW engines... Of course, we had Sta-Tites installed."

If, some day, they pass you on a hill or beat you leaving a light, just remember that *all cars* are wearing out a little at a time all the time. Then maybe you'll go and get your Sta-Tites, too!

Buy Sealed Power motor parts where you see this sign

SEALED POWER — AUTHORIZED SERVICE

SEALED POWER
PISTON RINGS, PISTONS
PISTON EXPANDERS
PISTON PINS, VALVES
CYLINDER SLEEVES

Sealed Power Corporation Muskegon, Michigan. Please send my free copy of "How to Cut the Cost of Repowering My Car." Also send card entitling me to absolutely free Sealed Power Diagnosis which will indicate what MY car needs.

Name
Street
City   State

THIS BOOKLET **FREE**

Mogul Federal oil bearings

Never
how low
in price . . .
but always
How Good

There are two ways to build a motor car. It can be built to sell at a certain price —and the quality brought within that predetermined range. Or, it can be built as finely as possible, letting the price fall where it may. La Salle is built to this latter formula. It is built as finely as Cadillac knows how—and priced as low as the quality will permit. That is what makes La Salle so unique —for no car built to a price formula could possibly compete with La Salle.

THE CADILLAC MOTOR CAR COMPANY
DETROIT, MICHIGAN

La Salle $1175

PRICES LIST AT
DETROIT, MICHIGAN

La Salle not only delivers exceptionally generous gasoline and oil mileage—but all service charges are unusually low. Furthermore, La Salle is so soundly designed and so superbly built that it requires much less service attention than cars of lesser quality. Almost anyone can afford to drive a La Salle.

Monthly payments to suit your purse on the G.M. Installment Plan.

LaSalle

MODERN SCIENCE
VS.
CIRCUMSTANTIAL EVIDENCE

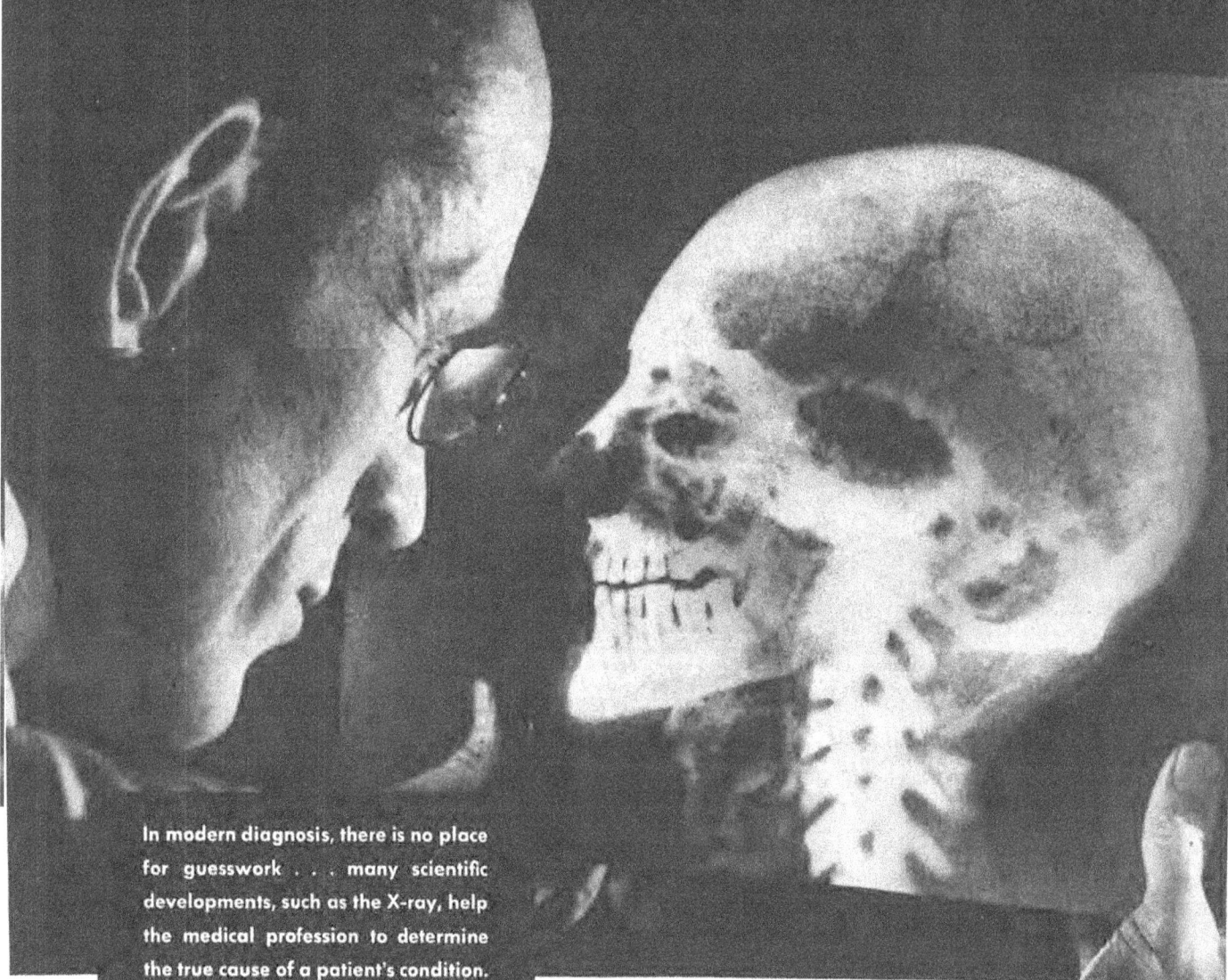

In modern diagnosis, there is no place for guesswork . . . many scientific developments, such as the X-ray, help the medical profession to determine the true cause of a patient's condition.

NEVER buy a new battery for your car just because somebody *guesses* that yours is worn out. A run-down condition is mere circumstantial evidence that a battery is worn out — and such evidence is not to be depended upon.

Good batteries, as well as worn-out batteries, run down. If yours runs down, find out definitely its true condition before you invest in a new one. And you *can* find out . . . quickly, without cost. The Exide Sure-Start Tester will tell you. It is a newly developed, scientific instrument that ends all guesswork. It shows the internal state of a battery as accurately as modern X-ray apparatus reveals to the surgeon certain physical conditions of the human body.

Go to a dealer displaying the Exide Sure-Start Service sign. He will gladly test your battery on one of these new instruments. If you wish, you may test it yourself . . . the test is easy, simple, quick, and involves no obligation.

Don't let guesswork — circumstantial evidence—condemn your battery. Get the facts on its real condition and protect yourself against needless expense.

ECONOMICAL BATTERIES

A wide price-range makes Exide dependability, economy and long life available to every car-owner.

WHEN IT'S AN *Exide* YOU START

THE ELECTRIC STORAGE BATTERY COMPANY
Philadelphia... *The World's Largest Manufacturers of Storage Batteries for Every Purpose*
Exide Batteries of Canada, Limited, Toronto

Exide batteries

Dodge Trucks

A hundred thousand tons of cars—people—merchandise—actually 42,231 cars—a single day's traffic across the George Washington bridge.

40,000 CARS A DAY

and safety taken for granted

● The oil in your crankcase . . . do you think of it as you drive? Hardly more than you think of the giant cables that support a great bridge as you cross it.

Yet that unseen oil means safety to your motor — protection against wear and heat and repair bills. And you *are* safe when you use New Pennzoil.

New Pennzoil—tough-film, heat-resisting, sludge-free — gives you perfect, safe lubrication always, with more power and improved performance. It lasts longer, too, protecting your purse as well as your power plant.

That's why Union Pacific streamline trains use Pennzoil — for power, for performance, for economy, for the safety of costly equipment. It's why over half the air transport miles in the United States are flown with Pennzoil.

That same New Pennzoil in your car will actually save you up to 50% on oil cost, up to 90% on valve and piston ring repairs, and give you an extra mile or two per gallon of gas.

Independent dealers everywhere are ready to serve you with the proper grade for your car.

Member Penn. Grade Crude Oil Assn. Permit No. 2

United Air Lines uses Pennzoil in the world's largest fleet of high speed transport planes.

BONDED PENNZOIL DEALER
100% Pure Pennsylvania
PENNZOIL
Safe Lubrication

LONGER SAFE LUBRICATION AT THIS SIGN

Pennzoil

"Great" AROUND A CAR!

Mobil Handy Oil
PENETRATES . . . STAYS PUT

SAFE FOR GENERATOR, starter or distributor . . . protects parts and body hardware against "dry" wear. Mobil Handy Oil, the new, specially compounded lubricant, penetrates quickly . . . cuts rust easily . . . yet stays put. Fine for tools, household oiling, delicate mechanisms. At Mobiloil stations and leading dealers.

Free—WALL CLIP WITH EVERY CAN
Keeps oil handy on wall of garage, shop, kitchen, etc.

Mobil Handy Oil

Mobil-Products
MADE BY THE MAKERS OF MOBILOIL

SOCONY-VACUUM

MOBILGLOSS • MOBILWAX • MOBILWAX PAD
MOBIL HANDY OIL • MOBIL RADIATOR FLUSH
MOBIL HYDROTONE • MOBIL UPPERLUBE

Mobiloil

Ramco piston rings

MOTORISTS-FREE

Buy these 2 money-saving items

FOR 89¢

LUSTRE WAX
(Reg. Price **50¢**)

WAX-PREP CLEANER
(Reg. Price **50¢**)

—and get this Goodrich Chemically Treated POLISHING CLOTH *Free*

Goodrich CHEMICALLY TREATED POLISHING CLOTH
CLEANS AND POLISHES AUTOMOBILES, FURNITURE, DUCO, LACQUER AND ALL VARNISHED SURFACES

A REGULAR $1.39 VALUE FOR ONLY 89¢

TO PROVE there's nothing like Goodrich Accessories to keep your car looking like new, your Goodrich dealer is making this Special Introductory Offer until May 31st. Think of it! You pay less than the regular price of Goodrich Wax-Prep Cleaner and Goodrich Lustre Wax, and you get the *chemically-treated* Goodrich Polishing Cloth (reg. price 39¢) *absolutely free.* Take advantage of this special offer . . . restore the original color and lustre of your car.

ANOTHER B. F. GOODRICH PRODUCT

Lustre Wax polish

THE NEW STUDEBAKER IS
AN OFFICIALLY PROVED
Gas Economy Champion!

$665 AND UP AT FACTORY, SOUTH BEND

A FEW DOLLARS MORE THAN LOWEST PRICED CARS!

NO MORE WISHING YOU HAD AN EXTRA LEG WHEN YOU STOP ON A HILL.—*Studebaker has an Automatic Hill Holder, the only car that has. You just hold the clutch pedal down. Car doesn't roll back. Your right foot is free for the gas pedal.*

STUDEBAKER has written a new economy prescription for the thrifty 1936 car buyer. It isn't necessary to confine yourself to a small car of very lowest price any more.

For almost as modest an outlay of money, you may have Studebaker size, style, stamina and brilliance of performance . . . with surprising gas and oil economy thrown in for extra measure!

Under American Automobile Association supervision, a stock Studebaker Dictator led its price group in the national gas economy classic in California earlier this year. In fact, the Dictator's official record of 24.27 miles per gallon excelled that of lowest priced cars in the same event!

Helen Dryden smartness in every lovely line! The world's strongest steel body and largest one-piece steel top! Feather-touch hydraulic brakes! Delightful roominess and matchless riding comfort! Studebaker prices begin at $665 for the Dictator Six . . . at $965 for the President Eight. And Studebaker's c. i. t. 6% plan offers a new low in time payments.

**OFFICIAL ECONOMY
RECORD 24.27 MILES PER GALLON**

This impressive record, set by a stock Studebaker Dictator Six in the National Classic in California, is certified by American Automobile Association.

**AUTOMATIC OVERDRIVE
MADE IT POSSIBLE**

In the above official economy test in which the Dictator scored so brilliantly, a stock Studebaker President Eight also led its class with an average of 20.34 miles per gallon. Both cars were equipped with the sensational automatic gas-saving Studebaker overdrive which gives you 3 miles of travel for every 2 miles of engine work!

Studebaker

SMART TO BE SEEN IN . . . SMARTER TO BUY

Studebaker

"My car rattles something terrible. Will MARFAK help?"

Let us **MARFAK** *your car*

"It certainly will. MARFAK'S so tough it won't squeeze out of the "joints" like ordinary grease does."

At Texaco Dealers, Texaco Stations and other places that treat cars right

NEW FULL-SIZE CHRIS-CRAFT CRUISER

Marfak

1938 ADS

Again

Cadillac s

PRESENTING – *A COMPLETELY*

CADILLAC ANNOUNCEMENTS are invariably the outstanding events of each new automotive year. But there has never been a time when it was so important to visit a Cadillac showroom as it is today. The new Cadillacs and LaSalles, now on display, completely sum up all that the world knows of luxurious, personal transportation. They do more. Each presents innovations in every department of motoring which point the way to progress for the entire industry . . . and each is offered at a price which sets the value standard for its field.

THE NEW LASALLE, for example, is *completely* new. Its brilliant new styling unites the best European practices with a wholly original new streamline treatment. The bodies represent an almost unbelievable advance in roominess, comfort, luxury, and safety. And the Cadillac V-8 engine, which powers the new LaSalle, is the smoothest, quietest and finest performing engine ever offered in a medium-priced car.

THE NEW CADILLAC SIXTY SPECIAL—the car which completely changed the trend of motor car design in 1938—and its companion car, the new Sixty-One—again have no competitors in their field. Leadership has been maintained by adding to all phases of performance, and by a remarkable increase in the richness of appearance and appointments.

THE NEW CADILLAC-FLEETWOODS—the V-8 and the V-16—further enhance Cadillac's reputation as the greatest name in the fine-car field. Motorists who want unlimited luxury, comfort, safety, and performance will find that these splendid new Cadillacs, improved wherever an improvement could mean an authentic advance, completely fulfill their desires.

You are cordially invited to make the thorough inspection which these superb new cars deserve. Your dealer is holding Open House for that express purpose. Why not see him today?

THE NEW CADILLAC-FLEETWOOD V-8

hows the world !

NEW LASALLE · TWO NEW CADILLACS · AND TWO NEW CADILLAC-FLEETWOODS

THE NEW CADILLAC SIXTY SPECIAL

THE NEW LASALLE V-8

Cadillac Sixty Special

Lasalle V-8

MEASURE ALL CARS AGAINST THE NEW LOW-PRICED PONTIAC SIX!

NEW SAFETY SHIFT GEAR CONTROL*

NEW SILVER STREAK BEAUTY

NEW ENGINE FEATURES

NEW SAFETY STYLED INTERIORS

NEW EASIER CLUTCH ACTION

NEW BATTERY LOCATION

NEW KNEE-ACTION FEATURES

IMPROVED CENTER-POINT STEERING

VENTILATED TRIPLE-SEALED HYDRAULIC BRAKES

MORE LUXURIOUS UNISTEEL BODIES

NEW INTERIOR ROOMINESS

NEW MORE POWERFUL GENERATOR

GREATER BEAUTY

MORE EFFICIENT OPERATION

EVEN FINER PERFORMANCE

SAFETY SHIFT GEAR CONTROL*

THAT'S THE SURE WAY TO PROVE THAT THE
Newest Thing On Wheels Outvalues Them All

More important new features than any other low-priced car ... more beauty advancements ... more performance improvements ... more additions to safety and all-around efficiency—that's a quick picture of what the up-to-the-minute Pontiac now offers at a price near the lowest! Safety Shift Gear Control* alone is enough to prove what any comparison will verify—that the big, thrifty new Pontiac Six *outvalues them all*. Safety Shift clears the front floor and doubles handling ease. Yet this optional feature* costs only $10—proof aplenty that you must see and drive the Silver Streak if you are looking for the most your money can buy!

TUNE IN ON KATHRYN CRAVENS—"*News Through A Woman's Eyes*"—*every Monday, Wednesday, and Friday, at 2 p.m., E.S.T., Columbia Network.*

PONTIAC MOTOR DIVISION, *General Motors Sales Corporation*, PONTIAC, MICH.

OWNERS SAY, "18 TO 24 MILES PER GALLON!"

PONTIAC RULES THE LOW PRICE FIELD!

GENERAL MOTORS TERMS TO SUIT YOUR PURSE

AMERICA'S FINEST LOW-PRICED CAR!

Pontiac Six   General Motors

LEAN BACK, BROTHER, AND LEARN SOMETHING!

That Easy Chair of Yours can Show You One Reason why the 1938 Buick has the Most Modern Chassis in the World

WHEN an easy-chair maker wants to build in comfort, what kind of springs does he use?

Right the first time — *coil* springs! Because coil springs are softer — last longer — keep their temper and springiness.

For such good reasons the 1938 Buick now has big, stout springs of *coiled* steel on all four wheels.

And by replacing the usual type of rear springing with TORQUE-FREE SPRINGING we not only gain a far smoother ride, but more constant traction, less wheel slip, lighter unsprung weight and surer car handling.

Buick is the only car that has such rear springing, and here's why.

Coil springs are not easily applied to any car that drives through the springs. Only a car like Buick, transmitting power through a torque-tube, can get full benefit of this new and better suspension.

With your interest in mechanical things, you'll want to inspect this new springing carefully and see how much simpler, safer and better it really is. You'll also find a lot to interest you in the *principle* of Buick's new DYNAFLASH engine.

Why don't you drop in on the nearest Buick dealer? You'll find the 1938 Buick has as many important new features as a red-headed kid has freckles.

NEW DYNAFLASH ENGINE

NEW TORQUE-FREE SPRINGING

USA 1938

WHEN BETTER AUTOMOBILES ARE BUILT BUICK WILL BUILD THEM

"Better buy Buick!"

A GENERAL GM MOTORS VALUE

Buick

General Motors

NEW DESOTO
IS NOW ON DISPLAY...
TED HUSING TELLS THE STORY

HUSING'S HIGHLIGHTS
OF A GREAT NEW CAR

★ De Soto's Handy-Shift — on the steering column — old "wobble stick" is gone.

★ Goodbye to "Trunk Bustles" — the Streamlined Luggage Locker is here!

★ Sofa-Wide Seats — front and rear — room for six big people!

★ 5 Speeds Forward! — with *Perfected* Automatic Overdrive — optional equipment on all models.

★ Full-View Windshield — higher, wider — with constant-speed wipers.

1 STREAMLINED STYLING is a fresh new note. Wide-range safety headlights *flush* in fenders. Most beautiful front-end you've ever seen on a motor car.

2 GEAR-SHIFTING IS EASY with De Soto's Handy-Shift mounted on steering post. Safety-Signal Speedometer shows green, amber, red... warns you of your speed.

3 NO TRUNK BUSTLE! Here's De Soto new Streamlined Luggage Locker Much bigger. 23 cubic feet of luggage space — but no bustle.

4 ROOM FOR SIX! De Soto's seats are as wide as a sofa! Room for 3 big people — front and rear. Plenty of leg room, head room.

5 NEW RIDE FORMULA! You enjoy a cradled ride. Rubber Float Body Mountings absorb vibration. Airplane-type Shock Absorbers smother bumps.

6 DE SOTO GIVES you BIG-CAR performance. Yet it's *priced just above the lowest.* See it at your De Soto dealer's! DE SOTO DIVISION OF CHRYSLER CORPORATION, Detroit, Mich.

SEE YOUR
DE SOTO
DEALER
FOR A GREAT CAR... FINE
SERVICE & A SQUARE DEAL

TUNE IN MAJOR BOWES' ORIGINAL AMATEUR HOUR, COLUMBIA NE WORK, THURSDAYS, 9 TO 10 P. M., E. S. T.

How Movies of Noise Gave Cars a "Hushed" Ride

REMEMBER the clatter of old-time "gas-buggies"? In today's Plymouth you can hear a watch tick! And it's priced with the lowest...with the Commercial Credit Company's easy terms offered by Dodge, De Soto and Chrysler dealers.

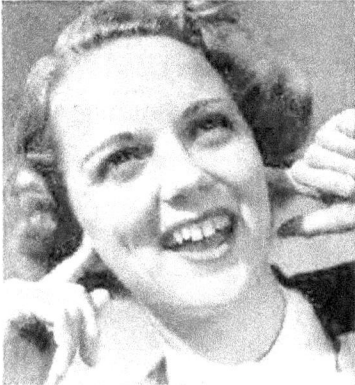

1 **This is One Way** to plug out noise. But Plymouth contains special insulating materials which effectively keep noise out...give a "hushed" ride!

2 **Different Parts of a Car** have different vibrations. So Plymouth engineers put microphones everywhere inside... to ferret out the slightest noise.

3 **They Used Television** tubes to photograph noise and transform it into light-rays. Throw these light-rays on a movie-film—and noise will paint its own picture for you.

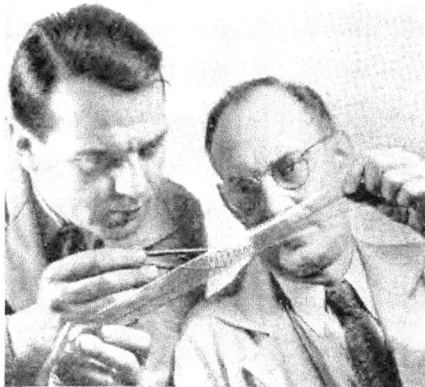

4 **This is a Movie of Noise.** Look at the wavering sound-track on the film. Plymouth engineers studied hundreds of these "movies." They worked out 5 different ways to stop noise.

5 **Dampens Hum, Rumble.** When you grab an alarm-clock bell, the vibration is "dampened." A special material dampens vibration in various Plymouth parts.

6 **Blocking Road Vibration.** Spools of rubber "float" Plymouth's body on the frame...efficiently block out road vibration.

7 **Soaking Up Noise from the Air.** Insulating materials are tested in this tunnel. Noise must be actually "soaked up" by these materials.

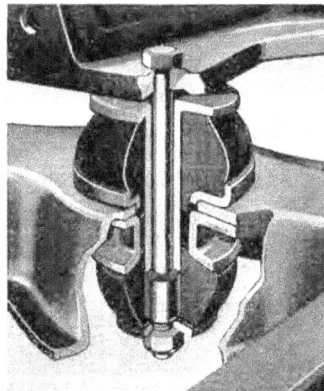

8 **Patented Floating Power** engine mountings keep power vibration from being telegraphed through the car's frame to the body.

9 **The Big 1938 Plymouth!** See it today—and learn the whole great story! PLYMOUTH DIVISION OF CHRYSLER CORPORATION, Detroit, Michigan.
Major Bowes' Amateur Hour, C.B.S. Network, Thurs., 9-10 p.m., E.S.T.

IT'S "THE CAR THAT STANDS UP BEST!" **Plymouth Builds Great Cars**

Plymouth

Chrysler Corporation

BUY
These Car and Home Specialties
NOW!

MOBILGLOSS

Polish your car with Mobilgloss. Takes off dirt, grease and grime quickly. Back comes the original color! Fine to prepare car for waxing. 12 oz. can.

MOBILWAX

Protects your car's finish. Goes on easily—polishes up quickly. In 3 oz. evaporation-proof tube.

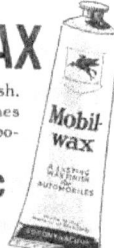

BOTH ONLY 69c

2 GREAT COMBINATION OFFERS!

MOBIL WINDOW SPRAY
AND HANDY SPRAYER

Don't spoil your hands cleaning windows! Mobil Window Spray needs no water. Spray it on—wipe it off—and windows sparkle! Special combination offer!

BOTH ONLY 69c

ON SALE AT MOBILOIL OR MOBILGAS DEALERS

Mobil Specialties

MOBILGLOSS · MOBILWAX · MOBILWAX PAD
MOBIL HANDY OIL · MOBIL RADIATOR FLUSH
MOBIL WINDOW SPRAY · MOBIL UPPERLUBE
MOBIL HYDROTONE · MOBIL SPOT REMOVER

BY THE MAKERS OF MOBILOIL

Mobil Specialties

The mass testimonial of
350 000
MEN AND WOMEN

"HYVIS is the finest oil I ever used!"

"The Mileage-Metered System puts me in the know about lubricating my car!"

"I get better service from HYVIS dealers —independents who know their business and own it!"

COPYRIGHT 1938 HYVIS OILS, INC.

Mileage-Metered
HYVIS
MOTOR OILS
SUPER-REFINED PENNSYLVANIA

HYVIS
Mileage-Metered
TRADEMARKS REG. U. S. PAT. OFF.

100% PURE
PENNSYLVANIA
OIL

Precision-refined by exclusive and protected processes. HYVIS Mileage-Metered Motor Oils are made only from supreme Pennsylvania Crude.

MOTOR OILS and LUBRICANTS

Watch These Speedometer Figures and Save

for **3**-figure mileage . . .	[up to ..... 999]	use HYVIS **3**
for **4**-figure mileage . . .	[from 1000 to ..... 9999]	use HYVIS **4**
for **5**-figure mileage . .	[from 10000 to ... 29999]	use HYVIS **5**
over **30,000** miles . .	[from 30000 to reboring ...]	use HYVIS **6**

(After reboring always count mileage as if car were new at that time.)

The reasons these thousands and thousands of smart motorists have turned to HYVIS are *real, honest-to-goodness* reasons.

You stop at a HYVIS sign and you know you have *automatically* picked the best independent dealer in the locality:—a local merchant who owns his own business, and who has the equipment, the skill and the special HYVIS lubricants to do the right job on your car.

And when you drive away, you know you have the world's finest oil in your crankcase. HYVIS oils are not by-products of gasoline manufacture, but oils refined from supreme Pennsylvania crudes,—the only oils of high enough quality to be precision-refined to Mileage-Metered standards. If you go longer between drains, you do so with ease of mind because HYVIS Mileage-Metered Oils *never break down.*

Add yourself to these 350,000 users! Your reward will be better, more economical upkeep—with greater gas and oil mileage. If you don't know the HYVIS dealer in your locality, it will be worth your while to write for his name and address. HYVIS OILS, Inc., Warren, Pa.

Hyvis Motor Oil and Lubricants

*Picturesque
Washington Street
Annisquam, Mass.*

Around to the drug store or away to a Picnic

Like clouds **DISTILLED!**

...USE DISTILLED OIL AND KEEP YOUR ENGINE CLEAN

If your engine is clean, you'll find motoring more enjoyable, whether you drive 5 miles or 500. And your engine will be clean if you use Havoline. For Havoline is distilled. Every drop of it is first turned to vapor to eliminate impurities.

An engine kept clean with Havoline has these definite advantages:

The motor is more responsive. It generates more power. It is faster on the get-away, smoother in its running.

You get more out of your gas. There is no hard carbon to cause knocking, your piston rings maintain their seal, your valves don't stick.

You are protected against the excess wear and repair bills that are often caused by the coarse, dangerous residue left by ordinary oils.

So why not join the millions of motorists who use Havoline and get more enjoyment out of their cars. It's easy to get —on sale at Texaco and other good dealers everywhere.

HAVOLINE
MOTOR OIL
WAXFREE

INDIAN REFINING COMPANY, INDIANAPOLIS, *affiliated with* THE TEXAS COMPANY

Copyright 1938, Indian Refining Company

Havoline Motor Oil

PLYMOUTH'S THE CAR!

"So Beautiful You Won't Believe It's a Low-Priced Car!"

GLAMOROUS NEW DISTINCTION IN STYLING...Lavish New Luxury...Longer Wheelbase...New High-Torque Engine Performance...Perfected Remote Control Shifting with New All-Silent Auto-Mesh Transmission ...New Amola Steel Coil Springs...New "Safety Signal" Speedometer.

PERFECTED REMOTE CONTROL GEAR SHIFT

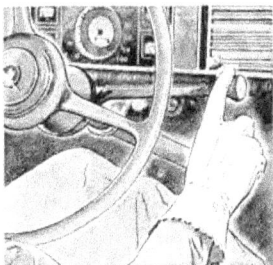

—with All-Silent Auto-Mesh Transmission, standard on De Luxe models. Nothing new to learn.

A DIFFERENT KIND OF RIDING COMFORT

New Amola Steel Coil Springs, finest springing design in industry. Amola Steel is the new marvel of metallurgy.

NEW "SAFETY SIGNAL" SPEEDOMETER

Indicator Light shows green up to 30 miles per hour...from 30 to 50, amber ...above 50, a warning red.

THE BEAUTIFUL NEW PLYMOUTH FOR 1939 now on display at your nearby Plymouth dealer. See it, ride in it, drive it, today!

A NEW "ROADKING"...AND A NEW "DE LUXE"...GREAT NEW VALUES!

SEE WHAT IT IS that makes Plymouth the car of the year: New, sweeping lines, the last word in style...new design headlamps giving greatly increased road lighting...new luxury interiors, great roominess!

Ride in this great Plymouth...drive it and experience the soft, new riding ease of its new Amola Steel Coil Springs, patented Floating Power engine mountings and 100% hydraulic, double-action brakes.

New True-Steady steering requires 15% less effort. Clutch and brake pedal pressure have been reduced. This new Plymouth is the easiest-handling car you ever drove!

And for 1939, Plymouth has thrilling new High-Torque engine performance...with new all-round economy!

Remarkably easy to own...your present car will probably represent a large proportion of Plymouth's low delivered price...balance in surprisingly low monthly instalments. See your nearby Plymouth dealer today. PLYMOUTH DIVISION OF CHRYSLER CORPORATION, Detroit, Michigan.

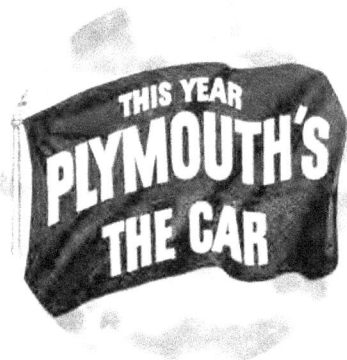

THIS YEAR PLYMOUTH'S THE CAR

PLYMOUTH BUILDS GREAT CARS

PLYMOUTH "ROADKING" 5-PASSENGER SEDAN

$685

—"Detroit delivered price," including front and rear bumpers and bumper guards, spare wheel, tire and tube, foot control for headlight beam with indicator on instrument panel, ash-tray front and rear, sun visor, safety glass and big trunk space (19.3 cubic feet). Plymouth "Roadking" models start at $615; "De Luxe" models slightly higher. Plymouth prices INCLUDE ALL FEDERAL TAXES. State, local taxes not included.

TUNE IN MAJOR BOWES' ORIGINAL AMATEUR HOUR... COLUMBIA NETWORK, THURS., 9 TO 10 P. M., E. S. T.

Plymouth

Chrysler Corporation

THIS MAY UPSET ALL YOUR IDEAS
about Anti-Freeze

THIS anti-freeze story may startle you. It is directly contrary to long-established beliefs. Tests made over a period of seven years in 300 cars prove that "Zerone" makes a perfect mixture with water and that you lose little or none by evaporation or separation. Radiator losses are due mainly to *mechanical causes*—leaks, sudden stops, etc. Where there is boiling, the losses are of *the whole solution*—"Zerone" and water—and such losses are in about the same proportions as the original protection.

So, in the first place, use "Zerone" in accordance with directions on can or protection chart. Second, never assume that it's the water only, or "Zerone" only, that has been lost when your cooling solution is low. Check strength of the solution, and replace the indicated *combination* of "Zerone" and water. Otherwise, you may have too much protection or too little, affecting performance and safety.

The materials from which "Zerone" is made are so effective you need less for protection. Replacements, if any, cost you little. So you are wiser to start with Du Pont "Zerone." Remember, it's only $1.00 a gallon ($1.20 west of the Rockies). Du Pont, "Zerone" Division, Wilmington, Delaware.

DUPONT ONLY $1 A GALLON
ZERONE
Anti-Rust ANTI-FREEZE

Zerone Anti-freeze   Du Pont

Presenting

Above, the Standard Ford V-8 Tudor . . . Below, the De Luxe Ford V-8 Fordor

THE TWO NEW FORD V·8 CARS FOR 1938

We're building two new cars for 1938—the Standard Ford V-8 and the De Luxe Ford V-8. They are different in appearance, but they have the same mechanical excellence —the same 112-inch wheelbase.

People liked our 1937 car so well that they bought more of them than of any other make. We have improved on that car in the newly styled Standard Ford V-8 for 1938.

But some folks asked also for a bigger, finer car with the same Ford advantages in it. For them, we designed the new De Luxe Ford V-8.

The De Luxe Sedans have longer bodies with more room, larger luggage space and finer appointments. De Luxe cars are equipped with the 85-horsepower engine only. They give an added measure of motoring satisfaction at low Ford prices.

The Standard is even lower priced than the De Luxe. It has pleasant new lines and well-tailored interiors. It offers again a choice of V-8 engine sizes; the powerful "85" or the thrifty "60."

Two cars, two engines, two price ranges. Whichever you choose, you get the same fundamental Ford features. Whatever you pay, you get a car built soundly to serve well.

Ford V-8

"YOUR CAR IS REALLY THREE CARS IN ONE"

...say service managers the country over

IF ANYONE KNOWS HIS CARS, it is the car dealer's service manager. So we have talked with scores of service managers all over the country. What they say boils down to this simple fact: *Every car has three different grades of performance.* Here's why:

The farther you advance the spark of a modern car, up to the point of maximum efficiency, the more power you get from gasoline.

But the modern motor "knocks" or "pings" when the spark is set farther ahead than the "anti-knock" quality of the gasoline used permits.

Judged by anti-knock quality, there are *three* grades of gasoline: "low grade," "regular" and gasoline containing "Ethyl."

That is why your car has a device—variously called "distributor adjuster," "Octane Selector," etc.—for setting the spark for each of these three grades of gasoline.

And the performance of your car depends upon the grade of gas and spark setting, as shown below.

GUS RUSHNECK, service manager, B. F. Curry, Inc., Chevrolet dealer, New York City, says: "When the public understands that there are three grades of performance built into every car, we service men will lead happier lives. Sure, the cars will run on any gas...but a Chevrolet has so much more on the ball when you can tune it up for real top-grade performance. That means gasoline 'with Ethyl.'"

O. E. MOORE, shop foreman for W. B. Deyo Co., Ford dealer in Detroit, Mich., says: "Those of us engaged daily in tuning cars *know* that the grade of fuel used goes a long way in making our work stand out. We never fail to recommend gasoline 'with Ethyl' to a customer who expects the tops in performance. Then we know we can go all the way with the spark advance and still avoid 'ping.'"

WILLIAM E. KENNEDY, service manager for Triangle Motor Sales, Inc., Chrysler and Plymouth distributors, Lima, O., says: "We give both our new and used car customers the best performance and the most economical run for their money by tuning up their cars for gasoline 'with Ethyl.' "Our call-back, no-charge labor costs have been reduced over 50% because now our cars are tuned up for Ethyl."

YOU HAVE THESE 3 CHOICES

Poor performance
with "low grade" gasoline

There is no anti-knock fluid (containing tetraethyl lead) in "low grade" gasoline. Power is lost because the spark must be retarded to prevent "knock" or "ping."

Good performance
with "regular" gasoline

Most regular gasoline has in it anti-knock fluid (containing tetraethyl lead). The spark can be considerably advanced for more power without "knock" or "ping."

Best performance
with gasoline containing "ETHYL"

Gasoline "with ETHYL" is highest in all-round quality. It has enough anti-knock fluid (containing tetraethyl lead) so that the spark can be *fully* advanced for maximum power and economy without "knock" or "ping."

ETHYL GASOLINE CORPORATION, *manufacturer of anti-knock fluids used by oil companies to improve gasoline*

Ethyl Gasoline

YOU CAN DEPEND ON CHAMPIONS

For Sustained High-Speed PERFORMANCE

When Ab Jenkins recently broke 87 World's, International and American speed records, on the Bonneville Salt Beds, averaging 157.27 miles per hour for 24 hours, he wrote an amazing bit of history involving a methodical man and a carefully prepared motor.

In this astounding record of perfect engine performance—the most destructive service conceivable—Champion Spark Plugs played a vital part to perfection. Not one spark plug was changed throughout the entire run, nor in the run he made previously in which 72 stock car records were broken.

Thus once again the soundness of Champion's 27-year-old policy of constant and tireless research and engineering, applied to the only product manufactured by Champion, has been confirmed. This concentration has kept Champion Spark Plugs everlastingly ahead in performance and dependability.

Every engine performs better with Champion Spark Plugs because they are made with that one purpose in mind, regardless of cost. The same quality of materials and design, the same exclusive and patented features are used throughout the entire Champion line, right down to

the tiny spark plugs built for model airplanes.

Demand Champions for your car because you can depend on them. Dependable dealers everywhere sell dependable Champions.

CHAMPION

THE SPARK PLUG CHAMPIONS USE

CHECK AND CLEAN SPARK PLUGS WHEN YOU CHANGE OIL

Champion spark plugs

FOUND:
SILENCE FOR MILLIONS OF CARS

"WHAT?_ MOBILGREASE STOPPED ALL THOSE SQUEAKS?"

MOBILGREASE
ENDS THEIR BODY SQUEAKS

MOBILGREASE gives new resistance to water—pressure—heat! Stays on the job every minute... stopping squeaks, wear...making cars ride easier!

That's why Mobilgrease has won 2½ *million new users* in the past year. *And that's why it's best for your car!* Ask your Mobiloil dealer about Mobilgrease.

"IF MOBILGREASE IS USED BY MILLIONS..IT MUST BE BEST FOR MY CAR, TOO!"

Mobil SOCONY-VACUUM **Lubrication**

COSTS NO MORE THAN AN ORDINARY GREASE JOB

Mobil Lubrication

Introducing the Revolutionary

NEW

SEIBERLING

SAFETY **S** TIRE

A TIRE BUILT ON
ENTIRELY NEW SAFETY PRINCIPLES!

1 "SAW-TOOTH" claws dig into the road when you apply the brakes . . . stop you quickly and safely! • • •

This unusual tire runs as quietly as a panther, as long as your foot is on the accelerator. But the instant you say, "Stop!" this unique tread *sticks out its claws!*

Touch your brakes, and those saw-toothed claws *dig* into the road *from every angle.* And they keep on doing it month after month because those "saw-teeth" go right to the bottom of the tread.

If you want to feel perfectly safe in "skiddy" weather, put these *new* Seiberlings on your car.

2 PATENTED SHOULDER VENTS dispel internal heat at blowout danger point, give you more mileage, more safety!

Here is the only tire in America that actually EXPELS the heat that causes most blowouts. Along its side-walls, patented vents reach down through the shoulder to the very vitals of the tire. As the car rolls along, these vents alternately open and close under the weight of the car . . . pumping hot air *out* and pulling cool air *into* the heart of the tire. Protect yourself against the blowout hazard by putting these new Safety Tires on your car NOW!

IT'S HEAT-VENTED

FOUR ADDITIONAL ADVANTAGES POSSESSED BY NO OTHER TIRE!

"Heat-proofed" Body – This is the first passenger car tire ever built of the newly-developed "Saf-flex" cord, –enables the tire to absorb terrific punishment and withstand the heat of high speed flexing–tire is as tough inside as outside!

Affinite Tread Compound –As different from ordinary tread compounds as solid mahogany is from soft

pine. Produces extremely dense tread rubber – makes tire wear like iron.

Vapor Cure–Patented Seiberling curing system assures 100% uniform quality. No soft, undercured tires– no brittle overbaked treads–means extra long life.

Streamlined beauty–Styled by a modern designer to be the "smartest-looking" tire that ever dressed up a car.

WARNING TO ALL MOTORISTS!
Look Out for this Criminal!

"Baldy" is a fiendish thug–lurking, perhaps, under the fenders of your automobile. During wet, slippery weather he has a habit of tossing car and passengers into a nasty accident in the twinkling of an eye. • Look under your fenders NOW! Get rid of your "Baldys" (smooth tires) . . . they're a constant menace to your life and your pocketbook.

"BALDY THE SLICK"

INTRODUCTORY TRADE-IN OFFER!

To introduce this sensational new tire, Seiberling dealers are offering *extra liberal trade-ins on your old tires NOW!* See the dealer nearest you!

THE SEIBERLING RUBBER COMPANY • AKRON, OHIO, U. S. A.
Seiberling Rubber Company of Canada, Ltd., Toronto, Canada

TIRES MOUNTED IN THE FALL AND WINTER LAST LONGER • *NOW* IS THE SMART TIME TO BUY YOUR TIRES!

Seiberling Safety Tire

DON'T GAMBLE with DEATH

Get a GRIP on the ROAD with . . .

WEED American
Bar-Reinforced TIRE CHAINS

● When the road is slippery with snow, ice or mud and you come to a busy crossing—*how do you know you can stop?*

Says the careful driver, "Because I have WEED American Bar-Reinforced Tire Chains—the chains that grip *three ways.*"

Equipped with Patented Lever-Lock End Hooks, WEED Americans are easier to put on and take off or to adjust. They are *economical* because, (1) WEED American Bar-Reinforcements provide twice the metal to wear through; (2) the metal is "Weedalloy," especially developed for WEED Tire Chain use; (3) side chains are welded and case-hardened to resist wear against curbs and ruts. WEED Americans give you *more than twice* the safe mileage.

WEED American Bar-Reinforced Tire Chains are offered by reliable accessory stores, garages and service stations.

AMERICAN CHAIN & CABLE COMPANY, INC.
BRIDGEPORT, CONNECTICUT

In Business for Your Safety

ACCO

See These WEED American Bar-Reinforcements • They stop FORWARD, BACK and SIDE Skids

WEED
WEED American Bar-Reinforced TIRE CHAINS

Licensed to manufacture and sell Bar-Reinforced Tire Chains under United States and Canadian Letters Patent: American Chain & Cable Company, Inc.; The McKay Company; The Hodell Chain Company; Pyrene Manufacturing Company; Dominion Chain Company, Limited; and Pyrene Manufacturing Company of Canada, Limited.

WEED tire chains

PICTURE NEWS OF AN AMAZING BATTERY
THAT'S GUARANTEED AS LONG AS YOU OWN YOUR CAR

DRIVE FROM MAINE TO CALIFORNIA AS OFTEN AS YOU WANT
Think of it! The new Goodrich Kathanode Electro-Pak Battery is guaranteed not for just a few months, a few years or a few thousand miles—*it's guaranteed as long as you own your passenger car.*

ADDS TO LIFE OF BATTERY
A feature of the patented Kathanode construction is the use of specially designed Spun Glass Retainer Mats. These flexible mats prevent the loss of active power-producing materials from the plates—assure a free, steady flow of power for quick starts even on coldest days.

SUPER-POWER CAN'T ESCAPE
Goodrich Electro-Paks are the only batteries with the Power-Saving Top Cover. Protects exposed points. Locks out dirt, acid spray and corrosion. *Seals in* the Electro-Pak's *super-power.*

NOW! A GOODRICH BATTERY FOR EVERY CAR...EVERY POCKETBOOK
Regardless of how large or small a battery you need, see your Goodrich Tire and Battery Dealer or Goodrich Silvertown Store today.

Goodrich
KATHANODE *Electro-Pak* BATTERY

Goodrich battery

PLYMOUTH BUILDS GREAT CARS

YOU'LL BE AMAZED AT PLYMOUTH'S LOW PRICE

THE BIGGEST BUY!

CHECK VALUES among Low-Priced Cars—in Comfort, Beauty, Economy! Prove for yourself Plymouth's Easier Driving—NOW!

GET THE MOST for your money when you buy! When you look at cars—see what you *actually get!*

ONE LOOK will tell you how outstanding this new Plymouth is...how extra roomy and beautiful.

ONE SHORT DRIVE will demonstrate Plymouth's remarkable ride... its luxurious big-car comfort and amazing safety features!

OWNERS' FIGURES prove that Plymouth costs less to run than any other full-powered car. You save on gas, oil, tires...on every item of upkeep!

THE PRICE will delight you. Ask a Dodge, De Soto or Chrysler dealer about Plymouth's very easy payment terms. And be sure to see, drive, and compare this new Plymouth—*today!* PLYMOUTH DIVISION OF CHRYSLER CORPORATION, Detroit, Michigan.

TUNE IN MAJOR BOWES' AMATEUR HOUR, COLUMBIA NETWORK, THURSDAYS, 9 TO 10 P. M., E. S. T.

PRICES ON ALL MODELS

Delivered in Detroit, including Federal taxes. Local, State taxes not included.

BUSINESS MODELS

Coupe, $645; 2-Door Sedan, $685; 4-Door Sedan, $730.

DE LUXE MODELS

Coupe, $730; Coupe with Rumble Seat, $770; Convertible Coupe, $850; 2-Door Sedan, $773; 2-Door Touring Sedan, $785; 4-Door Sedan, $803; 4-Door Touring Sedan, $815.

For delivered prices in your locality, see your Dodge, De Soto or Chrysler dealer.

SEE THE NEW PLYMOUTH

INVEST IN "THE CAR THAT STANDS UP BEST"

Plymouth

"LET'S SEE THE NEW DELCO AUTO RADIO"

If your auto radio isn't working the way it should, drive into a United Motors Service station, where radio specialists will get to the cause of the trouble and remove it. They will also be glad to show you the sensational new Delco auto radio. They know, out of their own experience, that Delco is today's outstanding auto radio value. Two new and exclusive features alone put it in a class by itself—Delcomatic Flash-Tuning and the Delco Acoustilator. There are seven attractive models in a wide range of prices.

United Motors Service is a nationwide organization of selected independent service stations authorized to sell and service these products:

DELCO Batteries	GUIDE Lamps
HYATT Roller Bearings	DELCO Auto Radios
DELCO Speedometers	HARRISON Heaters and Radiators
AC Fuel Pumps, Oil Filters, Speedometers, Gauges	DELCO-REMY Starting, Lighting, and Ignition
DELCO Shock Absorbers	KLAXON Horns
NEW DEPARTURE Ball Bearings	DELCO Hydraulic Brakes

**LOCALLY CONVENIENT
UNITED SERVICE MOTORS
LOOK FOR THIS SIGN**

Surrounded by Safety!

NEW SAFETY INSTRUMENT UNIT BEFORE YOU

All instruments are grouped in a handsome unit directly before the driver's eyes. Only Oldsmobile offers this new and invaluable feature for "safety first."

NEW SAFETY DASH FOR YOUR PASSENGERS

Quick stops are safe stops in an Oldsmobile. There are no protruding knobs or control buttons on the beautifully grained, burled-walnut finished dash.

(Below) NEW AUTOMATIC SAFETY TRANSMISSION

Simplifies car operation—provides smoother, livelier performance—saves gas and oil. You drive with both hands safely on the wheel. Optional at extra cost on all models of the Oldsmobile Six and Eight.

NEW SAFETY INTERIORS FOR THOSE IN THE REAR

The back of the front seat is rounded and heavily padded. The robe rail is the soft-cord type. Sharp corners and projections are completely eliminated.

SAFETY CHASSIS BELOW

. . . with Knee-Action Wheels, Center-Control Steering, Dual Ride Stabilizers and Super-Hydraulic Brakes.

UNISTEEL TURRET TOP BODY ALL AROUND YOU

Oldsmobile Bodies by Fisher give you the protection of solid steel above, below and on every side . . . the safest type of construction known.

SAFETY PLATE GLASS

You enjoy the extra security offered by Safety Plate Glass in the windshield and in all windows, at no extra cost.

Step Ahead and Be Money Ahead!
DRIVE AN

Oldsmobile

THE SIX

THE EIGHT

Oldsmobile Six   General Motors   Oldsmobile Eight

GOODYEAR

THE NEW
GOODYEAR DOUBLE EAGLE AIRWHEEL
BUILT WITH RAYOTWIST

It OUTRUNS ANYTHING ON WHEELS

ONE glance tells you this smartly streamlined new Goodyear Double Eagle Airwheel is the handsomest tire you've ever seen.

But what makes it the most important tire news in 25 years is the use of *a new basic material* that endows it with matchless ability to outperform anything on the road.

This material — spun from cotton cellulose and like carbohydrates into an amazingly tough satin-like rayon cord—is called RAYOTWIST*, developed by Goodyear.

This new cord is so superior in every way that a four-ply Rayotwist-bodied Double Eagle will give you far longer service than a six-ply conventional tire — *with greater comfort in every mile.*

That is because Rayotwist's greater strength and resistance to heat permit the use of a tougher, sturdier tread that multiplies mileage to new distance records.

Its lightness and greater resiliency make a nimbler, softer-riding tire, so free from road-fighting stiffness that it actually *decreases gasoline consumption.*

This smooth-rolling beauty, built with either white or black sidewalls — is fortified against skidding by the famous Goodyear All-Weather tread in a new compact design that affords maximum grip and traction.

To the Double Eagle's incomparable comfort and wear, add the infallible blowout-protection of Goodyear LifeGuards*—the modern successor to inner tubes—and you have the most luxurious safety underwheel the world has ever known!

MORE PEOPLE RIDE ON GOODYEAR TIRES THAN ON ANY OTHER KIND

Goodyear tires

WANT A GREAT RUN
FOR YOUR MONEY?

IF YOU'RE THE sort of person who thinks of a motor car as something more than a means of transportation —quit looking around and settle down . . . in the driver's seat of a new LaSalle!

You'll get a great run for your money there, and no fooling—whether you measure your value in miles or smiles.

Just for the fun of it, get a LaSalle from your dealer—and try it out for yourself.

Note the lift to your spirits as you slide in behind the wheel and let your eye travel down that sleek-as-a-cannon hood. You know, even before you try it, that you can simply take aim and step on the trigger! You'll go out of there like a shadow after the sun.

And keep your eye on the speedometer! The motor's so quiet and powerful that it can get you into trouble before you know it. It doesn't even purr—it just performs.

Here's a million-dollar "ride", if ever there was one. It's not only the comfortable, easy, soft way in which the car carries you over the rough places. There's also the way it hugs the road and stays steady on the turns and curves.

You not only feel *comfortable*—you feel *safe!* And you can't imagine what this does to your peace of mind until you've tried it. It adds a hundred per cent to the pleasures of driving.

Here's another thing, too. Human beings being what they are, you'll get a kick out of the head-turning. Most of the drivers you meet will give you an I-Wish-I-Had-That-Car look. Maybe that isn't worth money, but you'll find it's a lot of fun!

Why not see your dealer today, and learn what it's like to take command of the finest thing on the highway. He has the car—if you have the time.

And the weather's just about perfect for a trip through the countryside.

A GENERAL MOTORS VALUE

LOOK AT LASALLE!

V-8 . 125 HORSEPOWER CADILLAC ENGINE

REMEMBER—More than half of all manufacturers have models costing more than a new LaSalle. So —before you spend above $1,000 for a motor car, you owe it to yourself to—LOOK AT LASALLE!

LaSalle   Cadillac

Here's the $1.⁰⁰ anti-freeze
you can put in this very day

Only 50¢ worth now keeps most cars safe down to 10° above zero!

MAYBE this is an "Indian Summer" day, when you're not even thinking of anti-freeze. But you *know* a cold snap will come. You don't want to be caught unawares.

Set your mind at ease now. Drive in to your dealer or service station today and have a couple of quarts of Du Pont "Zerone" Anti-Freeze put in your cooling system, enough for protection, say, to 10° above zero. Then let the cold snap come when it may.

Check the radiator solution from time to time, and when winter gets down to *real* business, add enough "Zerone" for lower temperatures. Scientific tests over a period of seven years have proved that radiator losses are chiefly mechanical, and that a solution of "Zerone" *and* water is then lost — not one or the other alone. With "Zerone" you get improved engine performance, due to better heat dissipation, and better pep and efficiency, due to prevention of rust and corrosion in a clean cooling system. Why pay more when you can get all this in a $1.00 Anti-Freeze ($1.20 a gallon west of the Rockies). See your "Zerone" dealer today. Du Pont, "Zerone" Division, Wilmington, Del.

Only $1.⁰⁰ a gallon — Made by DUPONT

Zerone anti-freeze

SMARTEST AUTOMOBILE IN ALL PLYMOUTH HISTORY

"So Beautiful You Won't Believe It's a Low-Priced Car!"

GLAMOROUS NEW STYLING…New Luxury…New High-Torque Engine Performance…New Perfected Remote Control Shifting …New Auto-Mesh Transmission…New Amola Steel Coil Springs …New True-Steady Steering…New"Safety Signal"Speedometer.

NOW—a low-priced car of real distinction… and this great Plymouth's roomy, all-steel body is completely rust-proofed.

A NEW"ROADKING"…AND A NEW "DE LUXE"…NOW ON DISPLAY

THE NEW 1939 Plymouth is the most beautiful, most luxurious car ever to bear the Plymouth name! Magnificently styled…the new Plymouth is a far bigger car with a great new ride that's a new experience to low-price-car buyers.

Equally important is Plymouth's new High-Torque engine performance with all-round economy.

And it's easy to own…your present car will probably represent a large proportion of Plymouth's low delivered price…balance in low monthly instalments!

See your nearby Plymouth dealer! PLYMOUTH DIVISION OF CHRYSLER CORPORATION, Detroit, Mich.

THIS YEAR PLYMOUTH'S THE CAR

TUNE IN MAJOR BOWES' ORIGINAL AMATEUR HOUR, COLUMBIA NETWORK, THURSDAYS, 9 TO 10 P. M., E.S.T.

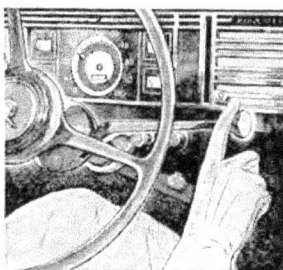

PERFECTED Remote Control Shifting, with All-Silent Auto-Mesh Transmission, standard equipment on De Luxe models.

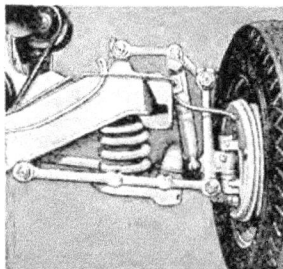

NEWEST DEVELOPMENT for your greater riding comfort… Plymouth's new coil springs of special Amola Steel.

SEE THIS SENSATIONAL NEW 1939 PLYMOUTH TODAY! Find out about its famed Floating Power engine mountings…and its 100% hydraulic, double-action brakes—the supreme product of 14 years' experience.

PLYMOUTH BUILDS GREAT CARS

PLYMOUTH"ROADKING" 5-PASSENGER SEDAN **$685** —"Detroit delivered price," including front and rear bumpers and bumper guards, spare wheel, tire and tube, foot control for headlight beam with indicator on instrument panel, ash-tray front and rear, sun visor, safety glass and big trunk space (19.3 cubic feet). Plymouth "Roadking" models start at $645; "DeLuxe" models slightly higher. Plymouth prices INCLUDE ALL FEDERAL TAXES. State, local taxes not included.

Plymouth Roadking   Chrysler Corporation

"WE TOOK A PLEDGE

Say Dodge Engineers,

"THAT'S WHY WE BUILT THIS SAFER CAR!"

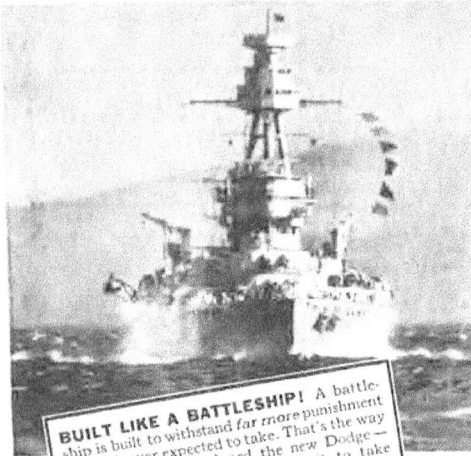

BUILT LIKE A BATTLESHIP! A battleship is built to withstand *far more* punishment than it is ever expected to take. That's the way Dodge engineers designed the new Dodge—built it to take built *extra* safety into it—built it to take punishment you'll never give it! See, in the pictures below, how they have done it!

RIGID DODGE FRAME SUPPORTS 6,000 POUNDS! If necessary, this double-rigid Dodge frame could support the weight of a 3-ton elephant! That's what Dodge engineers mean by the *extra* safety factor built into the vital parts of every Dodge!

NO "ROLLER COASTER" RIDE! New Dodge airplane-type hydraulic shock absorbers give you *added* safety on rough roads because, unlike shock absorbers on many cars, they control *both* the *upward and downward* motion of car! both front and rear ends of car!

SAFER! GENUINE HYDRAULIC BRAKES! Big enough to control a big truck if they had to! Nor do you have to "jam" them on to get the desired response. They bring you to a safe, even, non-swerving stop because the pressure on each wheel is *always* equal! Safety-sealed against water and dirt, they are always responsive on wet or dry roads.

HERE'S the car that motor experts and safety officials everywhere are talking about! The car that gives such a wonderful new meaning to safety that a prominent New York traffic official says: "It's the achievement of the year...the car that sets the pace for the future."

WHAT IT IS

It's the big new "Safety-Built" Dodge—and it was designed from the beginning to help cut accidents 'way down. In at least 15 important ways, it gives motorists greater protection against today's driving hazards. It's a sensational story...we can't begin to tell it all here...but we've put some of it in "words-and-pictures" for your convenience. Study these pictures! See for yourself why safety officials say, "*This is the safety car America has looked for!*"

No other car can give you all the great safety features that the 1938 Dodge offers. Imagine a frame so rugged it could stand the weight of a 3-ton elephant! Picture *genuine* hydraulic brakes that could control a big truck if they had to! Picture, too, genuine safety *plate* glass in *every single window!*...steel walls, steel floor and roof like a vault in the mint! ...and the big Red Ram Floating Power Engine with its *extra-fast* getaway to whisk you out of the tight spots!

MONEY IN YOUR POCKET!

But safety isn't all! Dodge owners say they've never driven a car that's so easy to handle...so gloriously comfortable to ride in. And the famous Dodge economy means money in your pocket every day you own it! Owners report 18 to 24 miles per gallon of gasoline—and up to 20% savings on oil!

And here's the best news of all! Dodge costs far less than many cars that do not give you as much...yet, remember this: it's priced so close to the small cars that you'll hardly notice the difference! See your Dodge dealer today! See and count *all* the great Dodge features which make up the 15 safety factors that are so vital to motoring safety today!

Tune in on the Major Bowes Original Amateur Hour, Columbia Network, every Thursday, 9 to 10 P. M., E. D. S. T.

SAFER WHEELS AND SPRINGS! Every week thousands pay to see Jimmie Lynch, daredevil stunt driver, put cars through the most fiendish tests ever devised! Look at the beating those Dodge wheels and springs take as Jimmie comes roaring off a "ski jump"! "I'd be a sucker to use any other car but Dodge," says Jimmie. "It has saved my life literally hundreds of times!"

BE SAFE IN THE BIG NEW DODGE

Dodge   Chrysler Corporation

TO SAVE LIVES!..."

DODGE ENGINEERS, who took a pledge to save lives by building Dodge safer in 15 vital ways: Fred M. Zeder, Vice-Chairman of the Board and head of engineering (fourth from left), and his associates: left to right, O. H. Clark, George B. Allen, Carl Breer, Mr. Zeder, Owen R. Skelton and H. T. Woolson.

BRIMFUL OF YOUTH! Vibrant, alive...loaded from stem to stern with zip and action...this new eyeful of streamlined beauty literally personifies youth! There's no engine back-talk here...when you say "go" to this car—she's GONE!

AND SAVE MONEY!

JUST A FEW DOLLARS MORE THAN THE LOWEST-PRICED CARS! Budget terms to suit your needs!

No Extra Cost

FOR GREATEST SKID PROTECTION YOU'VE EVER SEEN!

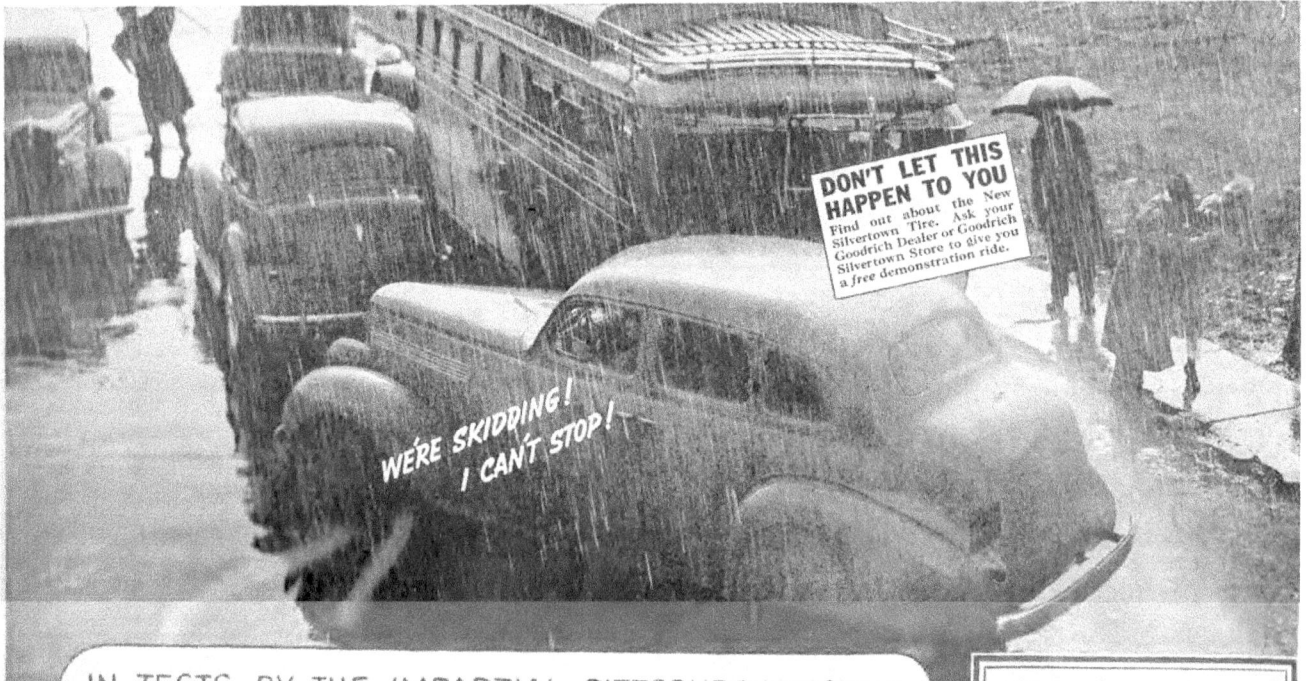

DON'T LET THIS HAPPEN TO YOU
Find out about the New Silvertown Tire. Ask your Goodrich Dealer or Goodrich Silvertown Store to give you a free demonstration ride.

WE'RE SKIDDING! I CAN'T STOP!

IN TESTS BY THE IMPARTIAL PITTSBURGH TESTING LABORATORY THIS NEW KIND OF TIRE GAVE QUICKER NON-SKID STOPS THAN TIRES PRICED UP TO 70% MORE!

LIFE-SAVER TREAD SKID PROTECTION

GOLDEN PLY BLOW-OUT PROTECTION

JUST *one* skid is usually enough to put the fear of wet, slippery roads into any motorist's heart. But here's a *new kind* of tire that makes wet weather driving *safer* than you ever dreamed possible—a tire that changes the rain-drenched road under your car from a "skid trap" to a *dry track!* It's the new Goodrich Silvertown Tire with the Life-Saver Tread!

How It Works

Next time it rains just notice the way your windshield wiper sweeps the water right and left to give you clear, safe vision. Pretty efficient little mechanism, isn't it? Well, that's how the amazing Life-Saver Tread on the new Goodrich Silvertown Tire performs on a wet road. In fact, the Life-Saver Tread acts like a whole battery of windshield wipers. It sweeps the water right and left —forces it out through the *deep* drainage grooves—makes a DRY TRACK for the rubber to grip—giving you the *quickest* non-skid stops you've ever seen!

And when you can get this real life-saving skid protection, *plus* Golden Ply protection against high speed blow-outs AT NO EXTRA COST why gamble on tires? See your Goodrich dealer or Goodrich Silvertown Store about equipping *your* car with these new Silvertowns with the Life-Saver Tread. Remember—*when it rains they stop!*

READ THE REPORT

from America's Largest Independent Testing Laboratory

"BOTH regular, and also the premium-priced tires of America's six largest tire manufacturers were submitted to a series of exhaustive road tests made over a three months' period by us, to determine their resistance to skidding and wear, with the following results:

"NON-SKID—The new Goodrich Silvertown with the Life-Saver Tread gave greater skid resistance than any other tire tested, including those tires listed at from 40% to 70% higher in price.

"MILEAGE—The Goodrich Silvertown gave more non-skid mileage than any of the other tires tested in its own price range—averaged 19.1% more miles before the tires wore smooth.

"BLOW-OUT PROTECTION—Despite the severe nature of these tests, no Silvertown blew out, or failed from any cause, while two tires of other makes failed."

PITTSBURGH TESTING LABORATORY

The new Goodrich SAFETY Silvertown

SKID PROTECTION OF LIFE-SAVER TREAD ❖ GOLDEN PLY BLOW-OUT PROTECTION

Goodrich tires

Goin' places?

Ask SHELL

FOR STATE ROAD MAPS
METROPOLITAN STREET MAPS
ACCOMMODATION DIRECTORIES

If you're going fishing—
**Shell can tell you how to
get to the best streams!**

Or if you're looking for new
golf courses to conquer—
**Shell can tell you where
they are!**

Or if you're just planning a
rocking-chair vacation in
the country—**Shell can tell
you the best places to go.**

WHATEVER your vacation plans
may be, stop in and see your neighborhood Shell dealer. He'll supply you
with maps, free of charge, and can give
you a good deal of helpful information
about routes and road conditions.

On the road, you'll find at every Shell
dealer's courteous service . . . home-
clean washrooms. If it's only your windshield to be cleaned, or free air or
water for your car, remember, wherever you are every Shell dealer is glad
to see you . . . ready to help you.

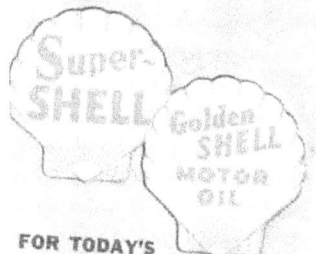

Super-
SHELL   Golden
SHELL
MOTOR
OIL

**FOR TODAY'S
STOP-AND-GO DRIVING**

Shell maps

ENJOYMENT of outdoor
pleasures and business rests largely upon the performance of
your motor car. Therefore, now is a good time to take your
car to the nearest Kendall Selected Dealer for the specialized
lubrication all late model cars require. Let him tell you of the
pleasure insurance and economy to be found in Kendall,
The 2000 Mile Oil. Millions of motorists have learned by
experience that it can be safely driven 2000 miles in any
weather, without oil change, by merely maintaining the oil
level. It is refined 100% from the world's choicest (Bradford,
Pennsylvania) crude. It is sold only in refinery sealed
cans, each numbered and registered for quality protection.

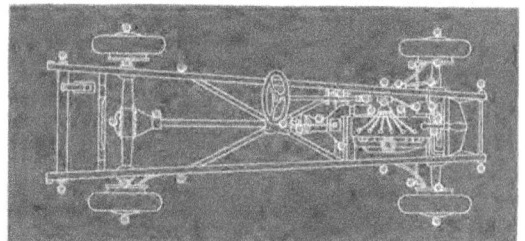

SAFETY, ease of handling and riding comfort depend upon thorough chassis
lubrication. There are more than 40 vital parts that require periodic attention.
A good chassis lubricant must resist mud, dust and the smack of splashing
water. It must give the safety of easy steering. It must insure riding comfort by its ability to withstand the millions of shackle shocks that occur
between each greasing. Kendall Chassis Lube has, as its lubricating base,
a highly refined heavy-bodied aircraft oil made 100% from Bradford, Pennsylvania crude oil. It is compounded into a tough, tenacious, water-resistant
grease in keeping with the high quality standards of all Kendall products.

KENDALL REFINING COMPANY · BRADFORD, PENNA.   ·   KENDALL REF. CO. OF CANADA LTD. TORONTO

Kendall oil

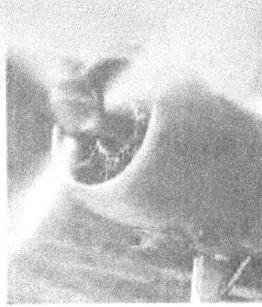

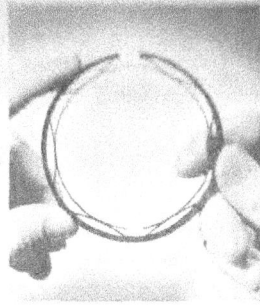

Perfect Circle piston rings

4-Wheel Brakes....Yes!

All-Steel Body...Certainly!

Safety Glass....Of Course!

Now.. for complete mo

GOODYEAR

YOU WOULDN'T THINK of driving a car today without 4-wheel brakes . . . all-steel body . . . or safety glass.

Yet necessary as these things are, they cannot save you if a tire suddenly fails. It takes Goodyear LifeGuards to make your motoring safety really complete.

There is no such thing as a blowout-proof tire! In spite of many millions of dollars spent in research and experiment, neither Goodyear nor any other tire builder can eliminate the possibility of high speed tire failure.

But you can be safe . . . by replacing the conventional tubes in your tires with

Goodyear LifeGuards. They take the danger out of blowouts, no matter how fast you drive . . . *no matter how old your tires are.*

LifeGuards are needed in all tires. But the older your tires get, the more important LifeGuards become. They enable you to get the *full life* out of your tires . . . with safety all the way. They save your money . . . as well as protect your life!

Hundreds of thousands of LifeGuards in service have proved LifeGuard protection. In the hands of private owners . . . in the tests of automobile engineers, not one single LifeGuard has ever failed to provide complete tire safety.

Goodyear Lifeguard tires

oring safety equip with

LIFEGUARDS*

You demand 4-wheel brakes, all-steel body and safety glass to make your car safe in today's traffic. Now you'll want Goodyear LifeGuards to make your motoring *completely safe.*

For safety's sake, equip your car today with LifeGuard tires. They are today's most important factor in motoring safety . . . a safety achievement that climaxes Goodyear's 40 years of contribution to motoring convenience, economy and comfort. *Only Goodyear* can offer you this priceless protection.

* * *

LIFEGUARD is a trade-mark of The Goodyear Tire & Rubber Company, and is fully protected by patents. Goodyear LifeGuards are made for passenger cars, trucks, buses and motorcycles.

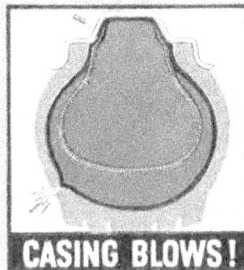

| CASING BLOWS! | TUBE BLOWS! | RESERVE TIRE SAFE! |

HOW LIFEGUARDS WORK: The Goodyear Life-Guard is a 2-ply *reserve tire* inside the tube . . . both inflated through the same valve. If casing and tube fail at high speed, the inner tire holds enough air to support the car until it can be brought to a smooth, safe stop. A LifeGuard-equipped car may be readily identified by the yellow and blue valve stems.

"SPARK PLUGS NEED CLEANING, TOO!"

Stop Wasting Gas...

GET YOUR PLUGS CLEANED

Oxide coating, soot and carbon collect on *all* spark plugs. They waste as much gas as one gallon in ten—and cause hard starting and loss of power. Plug cleaning costs only 5c a plug.

REGISTERED
AC
SPARK PLUG
CLEANING STATION

Official Plug Cleaning Sign
More than 70,000 dealers, garages, and service stations display this sign—because they clean and adjust plugs "by The AC Method." Look for this sign—always.

"Better let us clean the plugs, too. Dirty plugs sure cut engine power."

Modern engines demand clean plugs —and accurately adjusted gaps.

AC

When Plugs are Worn
Replace With
AC Quality Spark Plugs

30 years of quality spark plug manufacturing stand back of these newest AC products . . . assuring peak performance in all motor cars, trucks, buses, tractors, and power boats.

A C   S P A R K   P L U G   D I V I S I O N • *General Motors Corporation* • F L I N T ,   M I C H I G A N

AC spark plugs

For your family's comfort... and your car's beauty...
be sure the safety glass in your new car is
PLATE GLASS *not* WINDOW GLASS

ONLY PLATE GLASS CAN GUARANTEE IN EVERY WINDOW THE PERFECT VISION YOU GET THROUGH THE WINDSHIELD

Beauty
... No ordinary window glass, even though made by the most modern methods, can match the beauty of safety PLATE glass. Your car will look better with windows of safety PLATE glass—and that alone is reason enough for insisting on it.

Vision
... Genuine PLATE glass is ground and polished to a mirror finish. Because of this, PLATE glass alone guarantees you perfect vision from all angles. If you ride in back, you'll certainly insist on safety PLATE glass in every window.

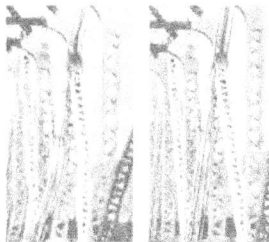

Comfort
... Modern shop windows are made of PLATE glass. Distorted vision is bad for eyes. Bad for riding comfort, too. Only genuine safety PLATE glass can give your family the comfort of undistorted vision.

No CAR MANUFACTURER puts ordinary safety window glass in the windshield. Only genuine safety PLATE glass can guarantee the perfect vision every driver needs. A majority of manufacturers now go even further and put safety PLATE glass in every window. You can quickly identify it by the quality mark shown in the photograph at the right. This mark is your guarantee of genuine safety PLATE glass, with the rich beauty and clear visibility that only PLATE glass can give you. Your new car will look better, and the folks in back will see better, if you insist on safety PLATE glass in every window. Plate Glass Manufacturers of America.

Safety PLATE Glass

Look for this quality mark on all windows

Safety Plate Glass

American Brakeblok

...BUT CAR-STARTING IS ONLY ONE OF EXIDE'S MANY DAILY SERVICES TO YOU

If you asked Bill Smith, an average business man, how often he uses an Exide Battery, he might answer—"Once to start my car in the morning, and again at night. About twice a day."

Let us follow Bill Smith and see. He drives to the station in the morning and boards a train for the city. The lights in the train and the signals that clear its path use batteries*.

He takes an elevator to his office—operated by a dependable supply of electric current that storage batteries* help to ensure.

If his firm receives a shipment from abroad, its passage was made safe by the batteries* used aboard ship to safeguard the operation of wireless and modern protective apparatus—while most of the trucks that handle the cargo on the docks are electric trucks powered by storage batteries*.

In one morning, he makes a dozen telephone calls—without knowing that batteries* help carry his voice over the wires.

That evening at home, Bill Smith turns on his radio. The broadcasting station uses batteries* to help keep its programs on the air.

Later, at a motion picture theatre, he hears the voices of the actors with startling realism—because the steady power of storage batteries* was used in making the film.

Asleep at night, Bill Smith and millions like him rest more comfortably because of the protection offered by municipal fire-alarm systems, for which storage batteries* are the source of unfailing power.

Like Bill Smith, all of us can take these services for granted largely because Exide Batteries perform their functions with such complete dependability. It is facts like these that can guide you in selecting the battery for your car. Is there any other battery which so thoroughly merits your confidence? Look for the Exide Dealer Sign—symbol of honest service.

THE ELECTRIC STORAGE BATTERY CO. Philadelphia . . . *The World's Largest Manufacturers of Storage Batteries for Every Purpose* Exide Batteries of Canada, Limited, Toronto

* Exide are the batteries that business and industry depend on in large measure for this and other vital services. To mark the fiftieth anniversary of Exide Batteries, a souvenir booklet has been prepared telling the complete story of the part these batteries play in daily life. Write, and we will gladly send you a free copy.

WHEN IT'S AN Exide YOU START

Exide battery

Saved from Acid Burns!

VAPORIZE! Down came a mist of acid . . . eating holes in clothes, destroying vegetation, ruining the finish of cars! "Luckily for me my car was Simonized," writes Robert O. Vernon, 1412 Sutherland Street, Los Angeles, Calif. "Although my car was covered with acid drops, not one cent's worth of damage was done to the finish."

I'M AHEAD THE PRICE OF A NEW PAINT JOB ON MY CAR...THANKS TO SIMONIZ!

KEEP YOUR CAR'S BEAUTY SAFE WITH SIMONIZ!

Every day the finish of your car is without Simoniz, it is in real danger! Even more dangerous than accidental mishaps are . . . weather, dirt and ultra-violet rays! Simoniz alone contains the secret ingredient which stops them from dulling and eventually destroying the finish. The protection it gives makes the lacquer and enamel last longer. In fact, your car becomes more and more beautiful. So, don't delay! Simoniz your car now! If the finish is dull, first use Simoniz Kleener. In one, quick, easy operation it thoroughly cleans and brings back the natural lustre your car had when new. Be sure to get Simoniz and Simoniz Kleener! Insist . . . and your car will always stay beautiful.

MOTORISTS WISE

SIMONIZ

SIMONIZ KLEENER

SIMONIZ

Nothing else gives the same results as Simoniz and Simoniz Kleener. They're inexpensive, easy to use and always dependable. Sold everywhere . . . never under any other name.

Simoniz car polish

HE TEMPTS FATE...
DELIBERATELY!

TIME TO RE-TIRE
"GET A FISK"

Blood-chilled spectators gasp as this daring stunt flier turns upside down only 30 feet above the ground ... yet they themselves every day take chances almost as great without even realizing it, for skids and blowouts are dangers that haunt the most skillful driver. Thousands of car owners are switching from ordinary tires to FISK SAFTI-FLIGHTS—"America's Safest Tires"—because Safti-Flights give them PLUS-PROTECTION against *both* of these menaces ... and do it *without extra cost.*

THE FISK TIRE COMPANY, INC.
CHICOPEE FALLS, MASS.
Copyright 1938, The Fisk Tire Co., Inc.

FISK

PLUS-*Protection* IN THE SKID ZONE ★ ★ PLUS-*Protection* IN THE BLOW-OUT ZONE

Fisk tires

A mile is only this far to your engine if you're driving in high gear

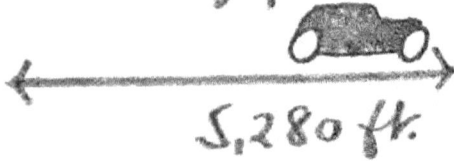

5,280 ft.

But in second gear, it's about this far

10,000 ft.

And in low gear, about this far

15,000 ft.

In **STOP** and **GO**, a mile S-T-R-E-T-C-H-E-S

In low and second, your engine makes up to 3 times as many revolutions as in high—*uses 3 times as much gasoline*

STOP-AND-GO driving fools your speedometer —while your car is going a mile, your engine may go the equivalent of *two*.

The number of extra revolutions your engine makes depends on how many times you stop and start—how much of your driving is in low and second gears.

You can't avoid stop-and-go driving, but you can do something about its high cost.

Shell engineers found that getting away from a traffic stop can waste enough "undigested" gasoline to carry you $\frac{1}{4}$ of a mile.

To cut this costly waste, they rearranged the chemical structure of gasoline. They make every drop of Super-Shell "motor digestible" —every drop usable in stop-and-go driving.

There is a Shell dealer near you. Use Super-Shell regularly and your savings count up.

SUPER-SHELL
SAVES ON STOP AND GO

SHELL

IT'S CALLED THE
"Roadking"
AND THAT'S EXACTLY WHAT IT IS!

☞ **IN "RIDE"** — This big, beautiful Plymouth has the most sensational ride in the lowest-price field.

☞ **IN SIZE** — Of the three leading lowest-priced cars, Plymouth is nearly 7 inches longer than one; more than 10 inches longer than the other.

☞ **IN POWER** — *Every* Plymouth model has the same big, 82-horsepower "L-head" engine...giving brilliant performance.

☞ **IN ECONOMY** — The "Roadking" saves money on gas, oil, tires, all upkeep. Get the facts.

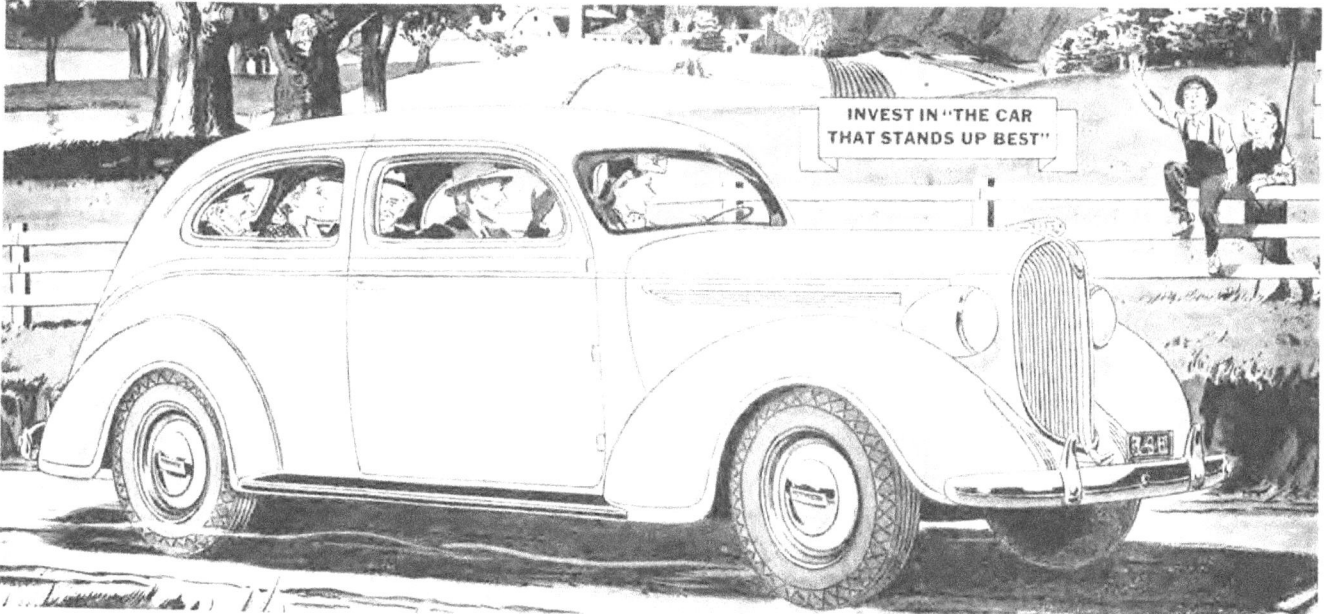

INVEST IN "THE CAR THAT STANDS UP BEST"

BEFORE you decide on any low-priced car, look at the advantages that Plymouth *alone* offers.

No other low-priced car offers this comfort: "radio studio" sound-proofing..."live" rubber body mountings...patented Floating Power engine mountings...big, airplane-type shock-absorbers.

No other low-priced car offers this safety: double-action hydraulic brakes...an all-steel body with a Safety Styled interior.

Take a ride in the big, new 1938 Plymouth today! Telephone your Dodge, De Soto or Chrysler dealer. PLYMOUTH DIVISION OF CHRYSLER CORPORATION, Detroit, Michigan.

PLYMOUTH "Roadking"
5-PASSENGER SEDAN
$685

Detroit delivered price. Plymouth "Roadking" models as low as $645... "De Luxe" models slightly higher. And Plymouth prices INCLUDE ALL FEDERAL TAXES. State, local taxes not included.

MAJOR BOWES' AMATEUR HOUR, C. B. S. NETWORK, THURSDAYS, 9 TO 10 P. M., E. D. S. T.

PLYMOUTH BUILDS GREAT CARS
THE "ROADKING"
THE "DE LUXE"

ENTER OLDSMOBILE'S NATIONWIDE PRIZE CONTEST

$10,000
IN CASH PRIZES

50 BIG AWARDS FOR THE WINNING LETTERS

1st Prize . . . $2,500.00
2nd Prize . . . $2,000.00
3rd Prize . . . $1,500.00
4th Prize . . . $1,000.00
5th Prize . . . $750.00
Next 10 Prizes, Each . . . $100.00
Next 15 Prizes, Each . . . $50.00
Next 20 Prizes, Each . . . $25.00

READ THESE SIMPLE RULES

1. Go to an Oldsmobile dealer and drive a 1938 Oldsmobile with Automatic Safety Transmission. The dealer will give you a Certificate of Entry, which contains the complete rules of this May Contest, signed by himself or his authorized representative.

Then write on your own stationery a letter of 200 words or less on "Why I Like Oldsmobile's Automatic Safety Transmission." Mail, together with signed Certificate of Entry, to Oldsmobile, Dept. C, Lansing, Mich. No letters will be considered eligible without accompanying Certificate.

2. Prizes will be awarded for the 50 best letters received during the period of the Contest. The decisions of the judges and their staff are final. In case of ties, duplicate prizes will be awarded.

3. Contest starts May 1 and all entries must be postmarked not later than 12:00 Midnight May 31, 1938.

4. All entries, statements and ideas therein become the property of Oldsmobile Division, General Motors Sales Corporation.

5. Contest open to any resident of the United States over 16 years of age except employees of Oldsmobile and its Advertising Agency and their families.

MORE THAN JUST A GEAR-SHIFTER!
OLDSMOBILE'S AUTOMATIC SAFETY TRANSMISSION OPENS UP A NEW WORLD OF MOTORING ENJOYMENT!

You've never tried anything like an Oldsmobile with Automatic Safety Transmission. It leaves other cars at the post when the signal changes . . . provides the smoothest, quietest cruising you've ever experienced . . . gives you a special Pick-Up gear for quick, safe passing . . . saves 18 to 20 per cent on gasoline. And it's easier, simpler and safer to drive. Try it today!

FOR THE BEST LETTERS ABOUT
OLDSMOBILE'S
AUTOMATIC SAFETY TRANSMISSION!

COME, GET ACQUAINTED with the greatest, most thrilling engineering development since the self-starter . . . Oldsmobile's Automatic Safety Transmission! More than just a gear-shifter, it opens up a whole new world of performance . . . makes driving simpler, safer and far more satisfying . . . saves money on gas and oil. As a special incentive to try Oldsmobile's Automatic Safety Transmission during May, Oldsmobile is staging a $10,000 Cash Prize Contest. To enter, you drive an Oldsmobile with Automatic Safety Transmission—then write a letter about it to Oldsmobile.

SIMPLE AND EASY TO ENTER . . . ALL YOU DO IS

SEE YOUR OLDSMOBILE DEALER

Ask your Oldsmobile dealer for a Certificate of Entry signed by himself or his authorized representative. He will also give you complete information about the operation of Oldsmobile's Automatic Safety Transmission.

DRIVE AN OLDSMOBILE WITH AUTOMATIC SAFETY TRANSMISSION

Put the car through its paces in traffic, up the hills, out on the open road. Get, at first hand, the complete story of this marvelous new kind of driving.

WRITE A 200-WORD LETTER TO OLDSMOBILE

Write on your own stationery and in your own words, the reasons "Why I Like Oldsmobile's Automatic Safety Transmission." Aptness, originality and sincerity count, not literary style. Even the simplest letter may win a prize.

CONTEST CLOSES MAY 31 . . . SEND IN YOUR ENTRY EARLY!

"It's Big! It's Fine! It's Beautiful!"

—SAY CHRYSLER OWNERS EVERYWHERE

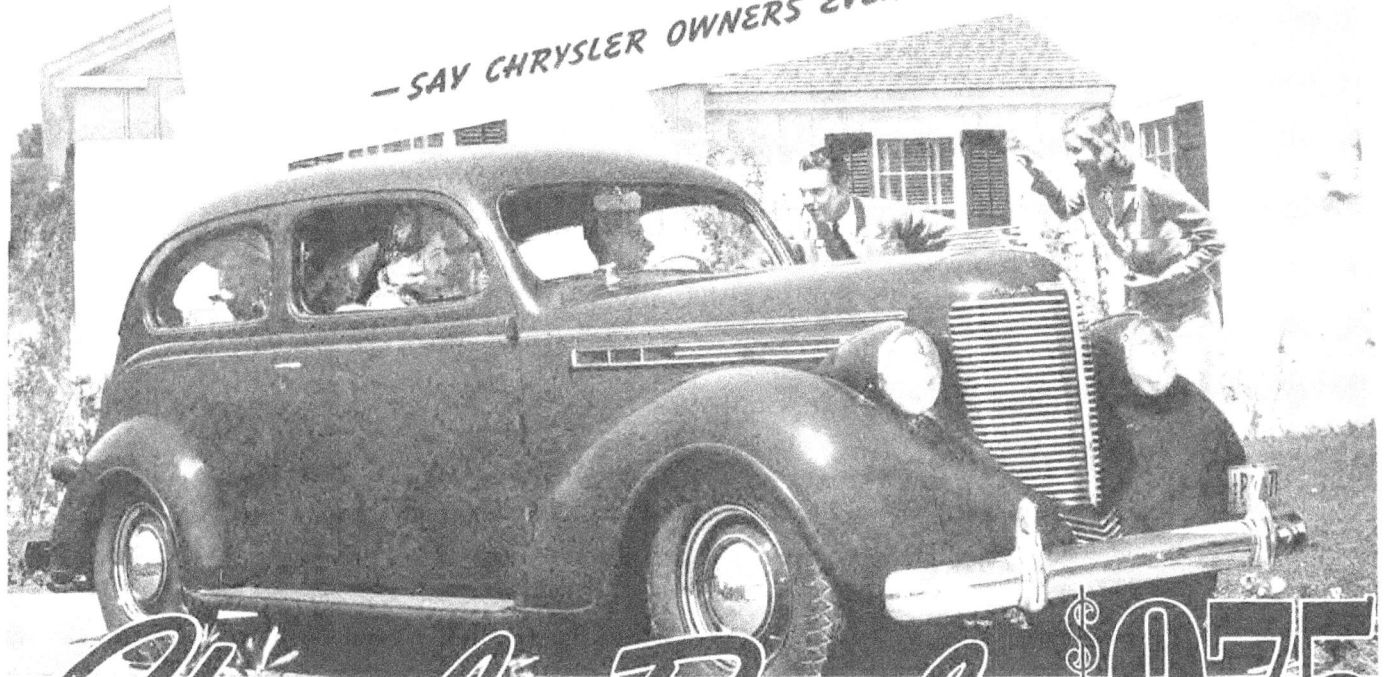

Chrysler Royal only $975

5-PASSENGER BROUGHAM
WITH TRUNK, READY TO
DRIVE IN DETROIT

Biggest money's worth in the low-
priced field! That's what owners call
the great new Chrysler Royal. Its
beauty . . . economy . . . engineering
and performance . . . are sources of
constant delight to owners everywhere. Read what some of them say.

★   ★   ★

Prices ready to drive in Detroit, including Federal taxes.

☆ CHRYSLER ROYAL . . . Coupe, $918. Four-Door
Touring Sedan with trunk, $1006. Eight other body styles.

☆ CHRYSLER IMPERIAL . . . Coupe, $1125. Four-
Door Touring Sedan with trunk, $1198. Four other body
styles.

☆ CHRYSLER CUSTOM IMPERIAL . . . 5 or 7-Pas-
senger Sedan, $2295. Sedan Limousine, $2395.
Above prices do not include state or local taxes, if any.
For delivered price in your locality, see your Chrysler
dealer.

☆ Tune in on Major Bowes, Columbia Network
Every Thursday, 9 to 10 P.M., E.D.S.T.

"Snappiest I've Ever Had"

"My Royal Sedan is my sixth Chrysler and
I've only spent $11 on all of them for re-
pairs, other than ordinary servicing and
adjustment. The snappiest car I've ever had.
I talk about its looks, performance and safety
all day. It has room for six big people."

HOWARD L. HEVERLY
Buffalo, N. Y.

"19 Miles per Gallon"

"Talk about economy! My Chrysler Royal
Brougham has extraordinary acceleration,
yet I average 19 miles per gallon at high
speeds. It's hard to beat for looks and its
extra roominess makes driving more comfortable. I'm very glad I bought a Royal."

OMER BROOKS
Cleveland, Ohio

"Best Looking Car of the Year"

"Everybody says my Chrysler Royal Sedan
is a beauty. It has exceptional power,
smoothness and economy. It rides like a
big, expensive car, but is easier to drive
and park. I'm very pleased with its safety
features and its big, roomy interior."

MRS. JAMES N. LOTT
Hollywood, Calif.

Chrysler Royal   Chrysler Corporation

"IT'S DYNAMITE IN KID GLOVES!
THIS IS MY THIRD DODGE"

says Warner Baxter

STAR OF 20TH-CENTURY-FOX'S "KIDNAPPED" By ROBERT LOUS STEVENSON

A DARRYL F. ZANUCK Production

READ WHAT WARNER BAXTER SAYS:
"I've owned three Dodge cars but my 1938 model is like a new kind of car—so much peppier and quick on the trigger. The first time I drove it in traffic, I was shocked—it gets away so fast! And it's loaded with power—but such a smooth, quiet power, you hardly know it's there. That's why I say this new Dodge is dynamite in kid gloves!"

VELVET SMOOTH POWER!

THANKS for the compliment, Warner Baxter. One ride and drive in this thrilling new car will convince anyone that your four-star praise of the 1938 Dodge is a deserved tribute...a fitting compliment from one great performer to another.

But who could help being excited about this car? Owners everywhere say you can't spend five minutes at the wheel of the big, new Dodge without getting a brand-new idea of riding and driving ease...a velvet-smooth power that you never dreamed was possible...a lift and a getaway that make just driving this sensational Dodge an exciting experience!

And wait till you see how she handles! You've never taken a wheel that does what you want so quickly, so smoothly. A touch of your fingers

guides her. And comfort? Man, sit back and relax in the smoothest thing on wheels. You could ride all day and step out at the end as fresh as a daisy. On sharp curves or straightaways...on rough roads or smooth, you'll say that riding comfort hits a new peak in this car.

Another thing you'll like is the famous Dodge economy. Owner after owner reports 18 to 24 miles to the gallon of gasoline, as well as savings up to 20% on oil.

BEST-PRICED CAR IN AMERICA!

And when it comes to price, Dodge is in a class by itself—*the best-priced car in America.* Here's why. Dodge costs far less than many cars that do not give you as much... On the other hand, it is priced so close to the low-priced cars that you'll hardly notice the difference! So why be satisfied with a *small*

car? Buy Dodge and get a big car, a greater and a car that will save you money every day, every mile you drive it. Don't wait—Get the whole amazing story from your dealer right away. Telephone him now! Budget terms to suit your needs!

DODGE
SWITCH TO DODGE AND SAVE MONEY!

This advertisement, DODGE Division of Chrysler Corp.

TUNE IN ON THE MAJOR BOWES ORIGINAL AMATEUR HOUR, COLUMBIC WORK, EVERY THURSDAY, 9:00 TO 10:00 P. M., EASTERN STANDARD

How to lead a dull life . . .

Never do anything just for the sheer fun of it. Never buy a thing simply because you want it.

For instance, pay no attention to the fact that you've always wanted a Packard. Don't bother to get any information. Say to yourself that a fine car like that just naturally *must* be out of your reach. Go on believing that it costs more to operate and service than the car you now own. Don't even ask the man who owns one.

Buy just any car. Keep telling yourself it's good enough—it runs, doesn't it?

. . . and how not to!

But if you like to get a kick out of life every once in a while—

—collect your wife and go down to a Packard showroom. Take one of the new lower-priced Packards out for a ride, and discover that never since you began driving a car have you ridden in anything that could touch it!

Learn that your old car will probably cover the down payment; that monthly payments are only a little more than those of the smaller cars; that operating costs are no higher; and that typical service costs are *less*.

Do these things. Then see if you don't end up in the driver's seat of a Packard—the car that will make life a little sweeter, you a little prouder, and driving a lot more fun.

Illustrated is the Packard Six convertible coupe

★ PACKARD ★

ASK THE MAN WHO OWNS ONE

Since the $100 price reduction on all body types of the new 1938 Packard Six—with no change whatsoever in the car itself—it is easier than ever to own a Packard.

See your Packard dealer for the figures showing the amazingly small difference in payments on a Packard Six and those on *much* smaller cars.

Packard Six

End your car's oil hunger!

Sealed Power Piston Rings work wonders with oil hungry cars. In fact, motorists everywhere report they've restored drain-to-drain oil mileage to cars that had used as much as 12, 13, 14 quarts between changes!

Twelve out of the 21 American makes of cars use Sealed Power Rings as original equipment. For best results, specify the brand factory engineers prefer—Sealed Power. Ace mechanics prefer Sealed Power, too!

SEALED POWER CORPORATION
Muskegon, Michigan • Canadian Factory, Walkerville, Ontario

Manufacturers of Piston Rings, Pistons, Piston Expanders, Piston Pins, Valves and Cylinder Sleeves

SEALED POWER PISTON RINGS

Sealed Power piston rings

PRICE SURPRISE OF THE SEASON!

WORLD FAMOUS
Studebaker Commander
$875

THERE'S a new blue ribbon winner for your motor car money this Spring.

It's the big, stunningly styled 1938 Studebaker Commander—now priced so low it's easy for anyone buying a new car to have Studebaker distinction.

What does it matter if you've only planned to buy a small, light car? You'll change your mind without an instant's hesitation, once you see how much the Commander gives you for a few dollars that you'll never miss.

The authoritative Magazine of Art calls the 1938 Studebaker the best designed car of the year. And a 10-mile trial drive will convince you that this great Commander runs more sweetly, stops more surely, steers more safely, handles more easily, rides more restfully, accelerates more brilliantly and climbs hills with less effort than any car you've tried.

What's more, it's built to resell at a top price years from now. You pay little down—balance on easy C.I.T. terms. The Studebaker Corporation, South Bend, Indiana.

$875 FOR THE 5-PASSENGER COUPE COMPLETELY EQUIPPED DELIVERED AT SOUTH BEND, IND. INCLUDING FEDERAL TAX

No other car, regardless of price, gives you all these Studebaker features at no extra cost

● Planar independent suspension
... The famous Miracle Ride
● Automatic hill holder
... No rolling back on up-grade stops
● Non-slam rotary door latches
... Finger-touch closing
● One-piece steel body reinforced by box section steel girders
... Battleship construction
● Fram oil cleaner and floating oil screen
... Better oil and motor economy
● Finest hydraulic shock absorbers
... Lullaby comfort

● Variable ratio steering
... Easier parking and better control
● Horizontal transmission
... Restfully level front floors
● Oversize weather-tight trunk
... Giant luggage capacity
● Front seat 55 inches wide
... Seats three comfortably
● Safety glass all around
... Indispensable protection
● Feather-touch hydraulic brakes
... Swift, sure stopping
● Hypoid gear rear axle ... Greater quiet

Front and rear bumpers, bumper guards, metal spring covers, two windshield wipers, fender tail lamp, license bracket tail lamp, sun visor, cloth upholstery, five painted disc wheels, extra tire and tube. *Vacuum-actuated Miracle Shift and Gas-saving Automatic Overdrive available at extra cost.*

Commander 6-passenger Cruising Sedan, complete with all equipment listed in panel at left, $960 delivered at South Bend, including Federal tax

Studebaker quality is in good hands!

Solid and sound in every inch is every Studebaker, thanks to workmanship that has no equal in the automobile world. Arthur Finch, pictured, is one of 5,000 conscientious long-time Studebaker craftsmen who keep bright the torch of quality that the Studebaker brothers lighted at the founding of the business in 1852.

Studebaker Commander

What your heart tells you about your motor…

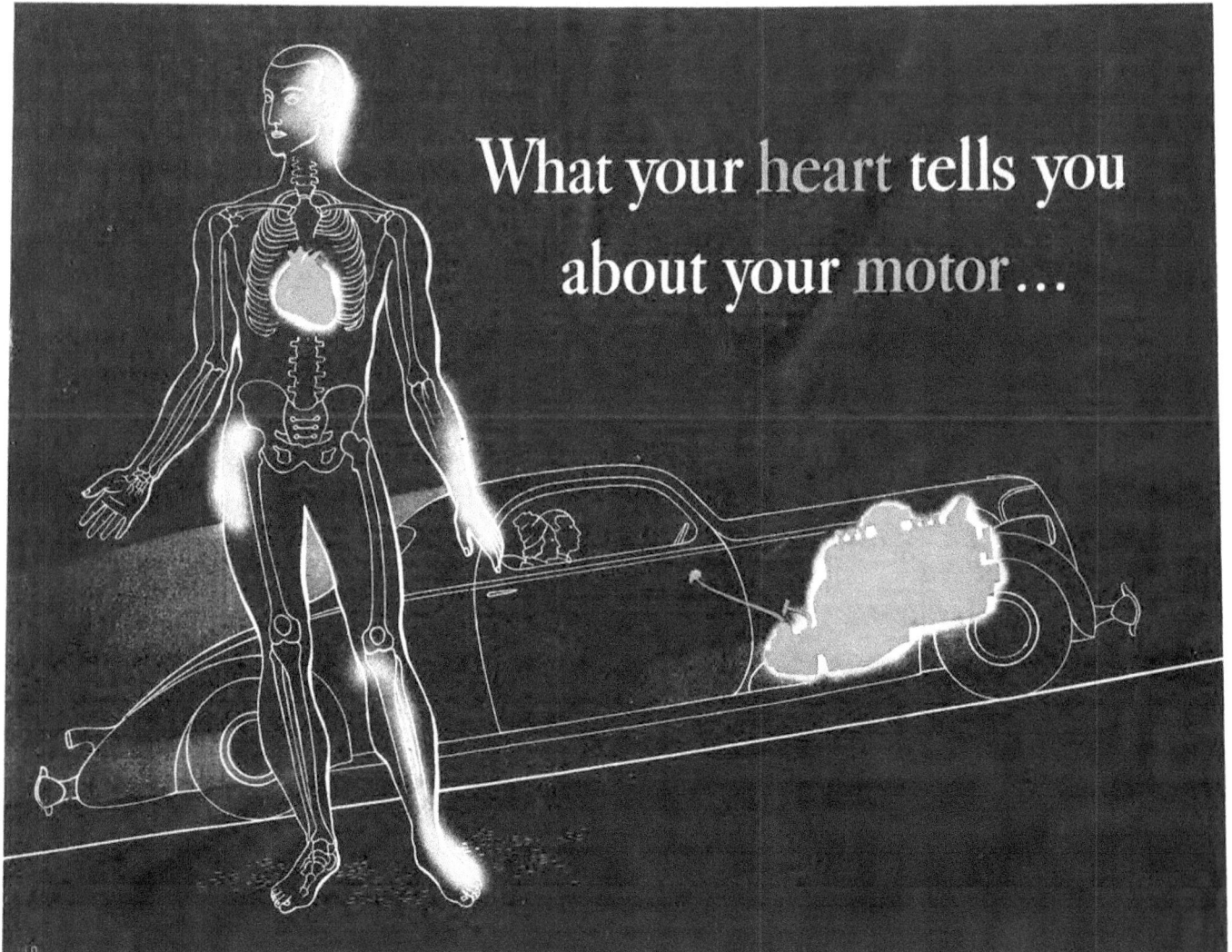

Your heart is a miracle mechanism beating at an average rate of 72 beats a minute. Nearly THREE BILLION beats if you live to be 75 years of age. But if FRICTION should occur in your heart …

Now see how wonderfully Nature guards your heart against the ravages of friction!

She encloses your heart in a sac called the *pericardium*. And between the inner wall of the sac and the outer surface of your heart a self-renewing film of lubrication is constantly maintained. Only the *thinnest* of films—*but of life and death importance!*

When any condition interferes with or breaks down this film of lubrication *the strain* upon your heart is multiplied many times over. Lubrication deficiency—Film-Failure—may make you a life-long invalid. Or even may be fatal.

· · ·

Be as considerate of the *motor* of your motor car as Nature is of your own *heart*. Don't neglect its lubrication.

Don't let your car become an invalid because of faulty lubrication—Film-Failure.

Loss of power is most always due to *Film-Failure.*

Sluggish pick-up is most always due to *Film-Failure.*

In extreme cases, the fatalities of burned-out bearings, cracked pistons and pitted valves have *Film-Failure* as the cause.

· · ·

You can guard your motor against Film-Failure by using *Veedol Motor Oil*, famed and acknowledged the whole world over as the *Film of Protection.*

Veedol is the "Film of Protection" because it is so nimble and fast-flowing. Even in the modern high-speed motor, it keeps every moving part constantly and completely lubricated and protected from heat, friction and pressure.

Veedol is the "Film of Protection" because it is

produced exclusively from the most prized crude on earth … Bradford-Pennsylvania. A crude endowed with elements of such positive and amazing character that its lubricating qualities must be compared with the perfect lubrication Nature provides for the human body.

Under the name of Veedol, this crude is refined by methods representing 60 years of continuous and progressive experience. Under the name of Veedol—and only under the name of Veedol—can you buy the "Film of Protection" for your car!

The Film of Protection

MADE FROM THE WORLD'S TOP-PRICE CRUDE OIL
YET NEVER PRICED HIGHER THAN 35 CENTS A QUART

Veedol motor oil

"Wrap up an extra quart," he says, "I'll use it on my wheat cakes"

No foolin', I never did a sellin' job as *complete* . . .

Mr. Phinney, he's got the build of a guy that don't miss the dinner gong, so when I told him his engine was starvin' for oil, he looked kinda sad and hungry himself.

I give him the works about Golden Shell—how it's made special for stop-and-go drivin'—how it gets up out of the crankcase in a flash when you step on the starter.

"*And the oil in your car ain't doin' that, Mr. Phinney,*" I says, lookin' sad, too. "It's sludgy and slow movin'! Your engine parts grind together dry before it gets goin', and that's where about ¾ of the wear comes."

He wiped his eyes, so I poured a drop or two of Golden Shell on my fingers.

"Lookit, Mr. Phinney," says I, "there's an OIL. Only 25¢ a quart, but feel the BODY. See the COLOR. Looks good, don't it?"

"Looks *good?*" he says. "It looks *wonderful!* Get that other stuff out of my car and put in Golden Shell. Say—"

I could see he was hit by a big idea.

"I tell you," he says, "wrap up an extra quart to take with me. I'll use it on my wheat cakes!"

You know, for a minute I thought he was serious!

Sincerely,

Your Shell Dealer

Shell gasoline

WE QUESTIONED

THOUSANDS OF TYPICAL CAR OWNERS TO FIND OUT WHAT KIND OF SERVICE THEY WANT WHEN THEY DRIVE IN FOR GAS

THA

FRIENDLY SE

It's the Service Mobilgas Dealers Know How to Give...and That Millions of Motorists Enjoy Today at the Red Horse Sign!

Mobilgas
SOCONY-VACUUM

D ID ONE OF THE SOCONY-VACUUM official investigators talk to you, too?

Our trained researchers talked to thousands of motorists...asked them "What kind of service do you want when you stop for gasoline?"

By an overwhelming vote, *we found the service they want is the "Friendly Service" that's made Mobilgas dealers famous!*

Isn't this the kind of service *you* want, too? Then drive your car into the next station that displays the Red Horse Mobilgas sign.

For Mobilgas dealers, from Coast to Coast, believe there is MORE...A LOT MORE!...to serving

MOBILGAS AND MO

THEY WANTED:
1. *WINDSHIELD WIPED*   4. *TIRES CHECKED*
2. *RADIATOR FILLED*   5. *REAR WINDOW WIPED*
3. *CLEAN WASHROOMS*   6. *FREE MAP SERVICE*

AT'S
RVICE

the motoring public than just filling up tanks with good gasoline!

Mobilgas dealers are glad to clean your windshield and rear window…fill your radiator, check your tires…maintain clean, safe washrooms for your comfort on the road.

Won't you bear this in mind—remember it—as you start your summer driving?

Wherever you go, look for the famous Flying Red Horse Sign. There's always one nearby. Stop in for Mobilgas, and for quick, thorough Friendly Service—America's favorite combination for easier, pleasanter driving!

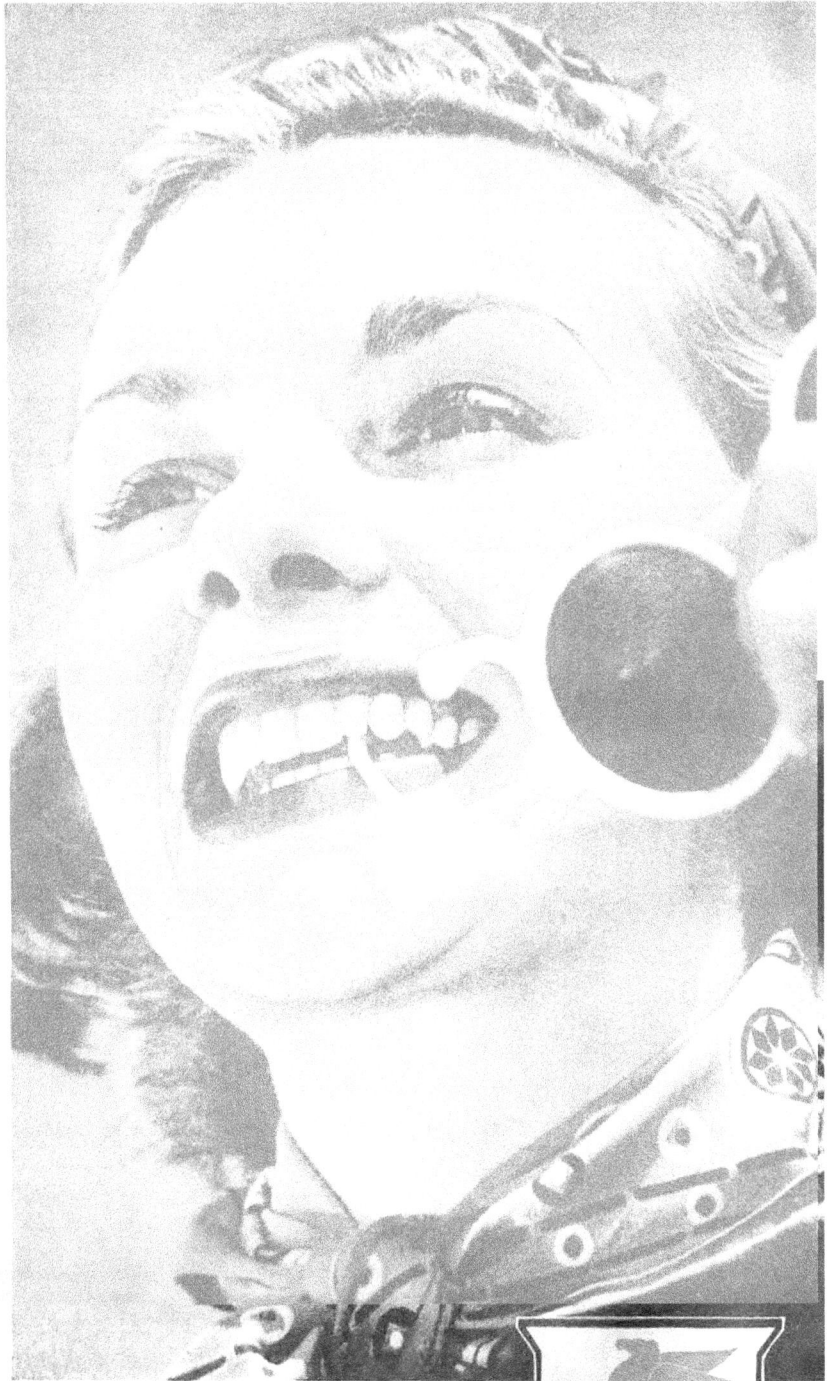

ILOIL SOCONY-VACUUM OIL COMPANY, INC.
AND AFFILIATES
MAGNOLIA PETROLEUM CO.—GENERAL PETROLEUM CORPORATION

Mobilgas
SOCONY-VACUUM

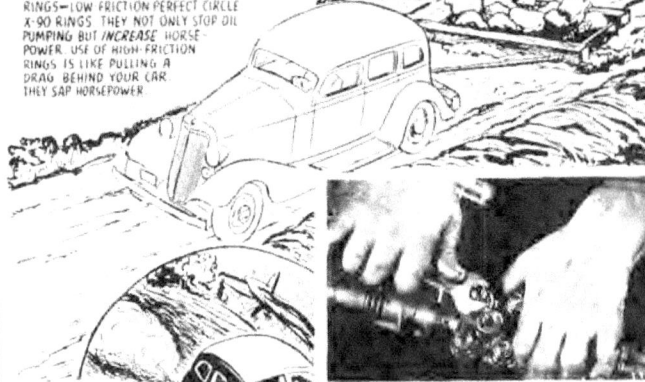

Perfect Circle piston rings

DEANNA DURBIN

ONE SMART GIRL
PICKS ONE SMART CAR

DEANNA DURBIN, STAR OF THE UNIVERSAL PICTURE "AD ABOUT MUSIC" IN HOLLYWOOD WITH HER NEW DE SOTO.

Read How De Soto Engineering Saves You Real Money
When You Buy—and EVERY MILE YOU DRIVE!

"I ENVY YOU YOUR NEW DE SOTO, DEANNA!"

"BUT IT'S SO EASY TO OWN DE SOTO IS NOW PRICED JUST ABOVE THE LOWEST!"

IT'S AMERICA'S SMARTEST LOW-PRICED CAR

1. Improved 93-H. P. "Economy Engine."
2. Safety-Steel Body.
3. Bigger, Genuine Hydraulic Brakes.
4. Luxurious Safety Interior.
5. Airplane-type Shock-absorbers.

TUNE IN MAJOR BOWES' AMATEUR HOUR—COLUMBIA NETWORK—THURSDAYS, 8 TO 9 P. M., E. S. T.

DEANNA DURBIN WAS SMART when she picked De Soto. She got the BIG CAR in the SMALL-CAR price class...the LUXURY car that costs no more to run than most SMALL cars!

It's true that De Soto's greater ECONOMY makes it good news in these days of careful buying. But you get much more than that—you get greater BEAUTY, greater PERFORMANCE, greater SAFETY in this BIG car that costs so little.

Drive De Soto yourself! Enjoy its faster pick-up...effortless steering...complete sound-proofing...the comfort of its new "cushioned" ride with airplane-type shock-absorbers.

De Soto is now priced JUST ABOVE THE LOWEST. See this great car today! DE SOTO DIVISION OF CHRYSLER CORPORATION, Detroit, Michigan.

SEE YOUR DE SOTO DEALER

FOR A
GREAT CAR, FINE SERVICE
AND A SQUARE DEAL

De Soto   Chrysler Corporation

PARTNERS IN SAFETY

Save a life

By KEEPING their cars tire-safe, careful drivers everywhere are doing their share in preventing thousands of accidents every year. With the men who enforce the laws, they form a safety partnership that will save many precious lives. Today, motorists by the thousands who want the utmost in tire safety are changing to Firestone Triple-Safe Tires because they demand three-way protection against tire failure.

PROTECTION AGAINST SKIDDING.
The scientifically designed tread will stop your car up to 25% quicker.

PROTECTION AGAINST BLOWOUTS.
Every fiber of every cord in every ply is saturated with liquid rubber by the Firestone patented Gum-Dipping

process. This counteracts the internal friction and heat that ordinarily cause blowouts.

PROTECTION AGAINST PUNCTURES.
Two extra layers of Gum-Dipped cords under the tread add strength to the tire and guard against the penetration of sharp particles.

Every driver owes it to himself and his family to join the Firestone SAVE A LIFE Campaign by equipping his car with a set of new Firestone Triple-Safe Tires — the safest tires that money can buy. See your nearest Firestone Dealer or Auto Supply and Service Store today. You will be amazed to learn how little it costs to make your car tire-safe!

Listen to the Voice of Firestone featuring Richard Crooks and Margaret Speaks, Monday evenings over Nationwide N. B. C. Red Network

Section of new Firestone Tire. Note protection against skidding, punctures and blowouts

Section of smooth, worn tire which is always susceptible to punctures, blowouts and skidding

Firestone TRIPLE-SAFE TIRES

Firestone tires

WE HANDED TH

TO OWNERS OF

Hudson 112 Six-Passenger Sedan, $755—fully equipped, ready to drive, Federal taxes paid—transportation and local taxes, if any, extra

"I still like you, Fuzzy, but I like our new car too!"

112-inch Wheelbase . . . 6 Cylinders . . . 83 Horsepower

$694

for 3-passenger Coupe; $724 for 6-passenger Brougham; $740 for 4-passenger Victoria Coupe, the only 4-passenger coupe in the lowest price field with all passengers riding inside; $755 for Sedan —fully equipped, ready to drive, Federal taxes paid—transportation costs and local taxes, if any, extra. Ask about the new lowcost Hudson-C.I.T. Time Payment Plan . . . terms to suit your income

TOP VALUE IN EVERY POPULAR

NEW HUDSON 112 • HUDSON *Terraplane* •
112 TO 129-INCH WHEELBASES . . . 83 TO

THE NEW "LOWEST PRICED"

IS NEW HUDSON 112 THE "OTHER THREE!"

WEEKS before the new Hudson 112 was announced, Hudson decided to put it to a most amazing test.

We didn't go to our friends. We didn't go to Hudson owners, or automobile men, or engineers. Instead, we went to the most exacting buyers in the world . . . *owners of the "other three" leading lowest priced cars*, whose names were furnished us by an impartial outside source.

We turned over to them *two* cars . . . the latest model of the car they already owned, and a new Hudson 112.

"Compare them," we said, "from roof to tire tread. Size, style, room, comfort, convenience, completeness, performance, safety, economy. We want *facts*. Just give us your honest opinions."

"NOW THERE ARE FOUR"
say owners of the "other three"
leading lowest priced cars

One of many safety features of the new Hudson 112 that owners of the "other three" particularly appreciated. The hood is hinged at the front . . . can't fly up and block the driver's vision if for any reason it should be left unlatched.

They Measured . . . Drove . . . Tested and Compared

AND THIS IS WHAT THEY SAID: (Names on request)

"I never saw such brakes! They work easily and give you a quick, level stop, sure! But what really caught my eye was that separate reserve set of mechanical brakes that operates from the same foot pedal. I saw a test when the hydraulics were disconnected and yet, when the driver pushed down on the brake pedal, the car stopped! From now on, that's the kind of brakes *I* want!"

"I bought my present car because I thought it would save me money. I was satisfied until I gave it an economy test alongside the new Hudson 112, and saw mine come off second best. If ever a car can pay its own way on gasoline saving, it's this new Hudson. That motor made a hit with me. It's not only smoother and quieter than mine, but it even seems to have more pep. Boy, that's a *car!*"

"With a family to look out for, I want a car that's safe, first of all. And I'll have to hand it to the new Hudson 112—it's the safest car I ever drove. I like the steel body, of course. The vision is much wider than in my present car. It seems to handle and ride more steadily. But best of all—those brakes! I've never seen any to compare with them."

"All I can say after driving this new Hudson 112 is that it's marvelous. I noticed right away how much easier it was to steer and handle than my car. And how much wider the vision is—as though you were in a box seat. You know there's always a sort of strangeness when you drive a car for the first time, but not in this 112. I felt right at home. Its beautiful streamlining will appeal to every woman's eye."

"I have been driving cars for ten years, some of them much bigger and more expensive than the Hudson 112, but none of them rode more comfortably or seemed to have any more room. I like the appearance of the hood and the modern design of the front end. I tried the brakes in heavy traffic, and they stop the car on a dime. All of my driving was in heavy traffic and the car handled perfectly."

"I thought I had all the room I was entitled to in my car, even for my 252 pounds, but that new Hudson 112 opened my eyes. It's wider, longer—bigger every way. That goes even for the baggage space in back and the parcel compartment up front. I thought my car was the best looking of the bunch, too. But now I'll have to agree that the new Hudson 112 beats it."

PRICE CLASS

HUDSON *Six* and *Eight*
122 HORSEPOWER

"NEW HUDSON 112 BIGGEST AND BEST!" is their verdict

'CAR HUDSON 112

A DASHING 1911 SPORT MODEL
(A Windshield was an "Extra")

When "Hitting 30" Was Reckless Driving,
an oil can provided "complete lubrication." And
"30" would still be fast if lubrication had stood
still. For a generation, Alemite has stood alone in
the development of better lubrication and better
lubricants for better cars. . . . That's why you'll

CUT DRIVING COSTS
BY DEMANDING
ALEMITE
REG. U. S. PAT. OFF.

Triple Safe Lubrication

THIS NEW safeguard against repairs—Alemite's
latest development in 20 years of lubrication leadership—lets you be *positive* that your car is lubricated according to its manufacturer's specifications.
Be sure your car gets this vital 3-way protection:

1 Your dealer who handles Alemite uses correct
   modern *Lubricants Created and Made by Alemite*

2 He uses special *Alemite High Pressure Guns* that
   force new, active lubricant to every point of
   strain and wear

3 A Trained *Alemite Service Man*—a man who
   knows and heeds every lubrication requirement
   of your particular car—does the work.

Have You Had Your Car Lubricated Recently?
Take It Now To A Dealer Who Displays This Sign

ALEMITE—*A Division of Stewart-Warner Corporation*
1826 Diversey Parkway, Chicago, Illinois
Stewart-Warner-Alemite Corporation of Canada, Ltd., Belleville, Ontario

ALEMITE
SERVICE

Listen to Heidt *Every Tuesday Nite*
A delightful musical variety program on Coast-to-Coast N.B.C. Network
9:00 Eastern Time   8:00 Central   7:00 Mountain   6:00 Pacific

Alemite lubrication

TWO WORDS HAVE SOLD FOUR MILLION TRUCKS...

FORD ECONOMY

ECONOMY has always been a major feature of the Ford Truck. That is the reason there are more Ford Trucks on the road today than any other truck. That is the reason more Ford Trucks were sold last year than any other 1937 make.

For 1938, the Ford V-8 Truck gives you still greater value. Again it writes ECONOMY on every cost sheet. Again it saves dollars because it does more work – in less time – at lower cost.

The V-8 engine puts the Ford Truck in a class by itself when it comes to work done. It means high sustained speeds – more payloads – more delivered dollars for every truck dollar. Only the Ford Truck gives you the extra speed and power of a V-8 engine.

And remember this important fact . . . Ford suits the engine to the job. The 134-inch and 157-inch wheelbase units are powered by the 85-horsepower engine. There's a choice of 85 or 60 horsepower in the new one-tonners and commercial cars.

The Ford Engine and Parts Exchange Plan is an extra time-saving, money-saving feature. A factory-reconditioned engine that will give new engine performance can be installed in your truck in a few hours. Factory-reconditioned parts can be kept on hand for quick replacement by your own mechanics. Your truck is ready for service more hours per month and your maintenance costs are less.

NEW 1938 FORD V-8 FEATURES

* New styling for all units.
* More comfortable cabs–3 inches more head room–handsome new interior trim – softer seat cushions.
* New 134-inch wheelbase, with 60-inch cab-to-axle measurement–improved load distribution.
* For 134-inch and 157-inch trucks, new standard frame width.
* Quicker stopping brakes.
* New larger spindles.
* Easier steering – new roller type with 18-inch wheel.
* 7.50-20 dual tire and wheel equipment available at extra cost.

ASK YOUR NEAREST FORD DEALER FOR AN "ON-THE-JOB" TEST

NEW 1938 FORD V·8 TRUCKS

Ford V-8 trucks

"We sell

Texaco gasoline

quick starts!"

We've got a gasoline for you that will start on the coldest day in less than 10 turns of the motor . . .

Here is good news for every motorist with an unheated garage . . . for drivers who park in the cold.

We can promise that our Texaco Fire-Chief gasoline will *always* start in *less* than 10 turns of your engine. No matter how cold. No matter how long your car has been exposed to zero weather.

What makes this promise possible? It is this: Introduced in 1932 as a new emergency-duty type gasoline, Texaco Fire-Chief has been continuously improved. Today laboratory cold-room tests fully prove its extra quick starting . . . its lively, economical winter performance.

So count on quick starts . . . purring "full power" delivered to your engine in 1/100th of a second or less . . . with Fire-Chief. Gasoline like this banishes cold morning uncertainty. Protects you from tow ropes and service cars.

Try a Texaco Dealer next time . . .

TEXACO DEALERS

Circle Service . . . a winter safeguard. In winter especially you feel more secure . . . more comfortable . . . with a sparkling clean windshield . . . clear headlights . . . assurance that your tires are properly inflated . . . and that oil and water have been checked. CIRCLE SERVICE gives you all this quickly, in one complete circling of your car. Thousands of Texaco Dealers are pledging it. Look for the Texaco sign as you drive.

Dependable

Sound engineering . . . fine materials . . . good workmanship . . . inspection at every stage of manufacture—all combine to make Delco batteries thoroughly dependable. This dependability is proved every day by the millions of motorists the world over, whose cars are equipped with Delco batteries.

Delco-Remy

MANUFACTURER OF DELCO-REMY STARTING LIGHTING AND IGNITION KLAXON HORNS · DELCO BATTERIES AUTOMATIC CARBURETOR CONTROLS

UNITED SERVICE MOTORS

DELCO-REMY PRODUCTS AND GENU-INE PARTS ARE AVAILABLE AT UNITED MOTORS SERVICE STATIONS EVERY-WHERE WHEREVER YOU SEE THIS SIGN

World's Largest Manufacturer of Automotive Electrical Equipment

Delco-Remy battery

Whatever You Haul

SMART APPEARANCE
International light-delivery units in ½-ton to 1-ton capacities, in three wheelbase lengths.

MANEUVERABILITY
International Cab-Over-Engine Model D-300—a new high standard for close work in crowded traffic.

LET INTERNATIONALS HAUL IT

You get the real measure of International Trucks only when they go to work for you. And then you get a better demonstration of stamina and economy—*more performance per dollar*—than you have ever known before.

International builds every type of truck to meet every trucking requirement, from ½-ton delivery to powerful six-wheelers. In all, there are 30 models in 99 wheelbase lengths. And every one of them is *all-truck* in every inch and ounce of construction and design.

Every International is engineered for outstanding performance and styled for brilliant appearance. The illustrations on this page show the quality of International design. For performance, let the trucks speak for themselves, for *your* business on *your* job.

There are 242 Company-owned branches and thousands of dealers *at your service*, ready to give you a demonstration at your convenience.

INTERNATIONAL HARVESTER COMPANY
180 North Michigan Avenue   Chicago, Illinois

CROSS TOWN OR CROSS COUNTRY
An International 3 to 4-ton Truck-Tractor. International Harvester sells *twice as many* heavy-duty trucks as any other manufacturer.

LEADER IN 1½-TON FIELD
International 1½-ton Model D-30 with special panel-stake body. Several other models for the medium-duty field.

STAMINA IN STEEL
There are many International Six-Wheel models, Dual-Drive and Trailing-Axle. Gross vehicle weights 18,000 to 62,000 pounds.

INTERNATIONAL TRUCKS

International Trucks

Mobilgas

CHOICE

The Winner: **MOBILGAS**
The Judges: **MOTORISTS OF THE U.S.A.**

YOU CAN TRUST THE SHREWD JUDGMENT OF AMERICAN MOTORISTS TO CHOOSE THE BEST GASOLINE ON THE MARKET

LADIES AND GENTLEMEN—THE WINNER! Again this year, the nation's 26,000,000 motorists choose Mobilgas as America's most popular gasoline.

Thanks for this vote of confidence! Thanks for your steady patronage!

We pledge ourselves to keep right on making the best gasoline your money can buy.

Mobilgas will continue to give you quicker firing. Smoother engine performance. Greater mileage. Extra power. Faster pick-up.

Because Mobilgas has *always* given the motorists of U.S.A. what they want...

A million and a half cars stop every day at the Sign of the Flying Red Horse!

Profit by their experience. Next time *you* need gas, stop at a Mobilgas dealer's...say, "Fill 'er up." Then step on the starter and learn what it means to pick the WINNER...learn why more motorists buy Mobilgas than any other gasoline in the U.S.A.!

MOBILOIL

SOCONY-VACUUM OIL COMPANY, INC.
AND AFFILIATES
MAGNOLIA PETROLEUM CO.—GENERAL PETROLEUM CORPORATION

Mobilgas
SOCONY-VACUUM

Mobiloil

"Mind wipin' the kitchen windows?" *she chirps*

In drives this old bus with a Tudor-Spanish villa hitched on behind. Before the driver can say howdy, a lady pops her head out of the bungalow and says, "Be sure and wipe the kitchen windows—and my garbage pail is full up."

So I empty the garbage and wash the windows, which gives me time to bring up my oil story.

"Stop-and-go sure takes it out of your engine," I start out, hopeful. "You park your trailer in a nice spot, and what does your oil do? Runs down in the crankcase!"

"Better be there than on the lawn," says the lady. I disregard her.

"When you start up in the morning," I tell her husband, "if your oil is sluggish—don't move *fast*—the engine parts grind together *dry*. You owe it to your home to use Golden Shell Oil!"

"We owe it to our home?" the fellow says, serious.

"You do!" I wind up. "Golden Shell costs only 25¢ a quart—a small price to pay in defense of your fireside!"

"Henry, get going," the lady chirps, "before this man sells you a battleship." And they clank out without spending a dime.

A woman can certainly make a fool out of you!

Sincerely,

Your Shell Dealer

Shell gasoline

On back road or boulevard . . . . there are

3 DIFFERENT GRADES OF PERFORMANCE
in your car

CHANCES are that you are *not* getting out of your car all the power its manufacturer put into it. You will be better able to know after you read these facts:

The farther you advance the spark of a modern high compression car, up to the point of maximum efficiency, the more power you get from gasoline.

But the motor "knocks" or "pings" when the spark is set farther ahead than the "anti-knock" quality of the gasoline permits.

Judged by anti-knock quality, there are *three* grades of gasoline: "low grade," "regular" and gasoline containing "Ethyl."

That is why your car has a device—variously called "distributor adjuster," "Octane Selector," etc.—for setting the spark for each of these three grades of gasoline.

And the performance of *your* car depends upon the grade of gas and spark setting, as shown below.

YOU HAVE THESE 3 CHOICES

Poor performance
with "low grade" gasoline

There is no anti-knock fluid (containing tetraethyl lead) in "low grade" gasoline. Power is lost because the spark must be retarded to prevent "knock" or "ping."

Good performance
with "regular" gasoline

Most regular gasoline has in it anti-knock fluid (containing tetraethyl lead). The spark can be considerably advanced for more power without "knock" or "ping."

Best performance
with gasoline containing "ETHYL"

Gasoline "with ETHYL" is highest in all-round quality. It has *enough* anti-knock fluid (containing tetraethyl lead) so that the spark can be *fully* advanced for maximum power and economy without "knock" or "ping."

ETHYL GASOLINE CORPORATION, *manufacturer of anti-knock fluids used by oil companies to improve gasoline*

Ethyl Gasoline

DO YOU KNOW?
By PERFECT CIRCLE

DO YOU KNOW...

THE LIFE OF YOUR **SON** OR **DAUGHTER** MAY BE SAVED BY READING THIS GREAT FREE BOOK?

SEND FOR IT TODAY.

DO YOU KNOW...

THE **SAFEST** THING TO DO WHEN YOU GO INTO A SHARP CURVE TOO FAST? SEE PAGE 56 OF FREE BOOK.

"IT'S LOW AGAIN"

STOP OIL PUMPING

AND RESTORE SPEED AND PEP WITH PERFECT CIRCLE PISTON RINGS. YOU NEED X-90's IF YOUR CAR HAS THESE SYMPTOMS. .1 EXCESSIVE OIL CONSUMPTION, 2.LOST POWER 3.BLUE EXHAUST SMOKE 4.FUMES IN CAR, 5. LOW GASOLINE MILEAGE.

SEND FOR FREE BOOK.

NEW STRAIGHT CYLINDER

WORN TAPERED CYLINDER

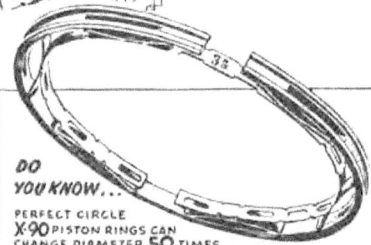

DO YOU KNOW...

CYLINDERS ALWAYS WEAR **TAPERED** CAUSING OIL PUMPING, LOST POWER, AND HIGH GASOLINE CONSUMPTION? THE EXTREME FLEXIBILITY OF **X-90** PISTON RINGS ENABLES THEM TO CONTACT TAPERED CYLINDERS AT ALL SPEEDS, SEALING AGAINST OIL AND POWER LOSS. SEE PAGE 30 OF FREE BOOK.

DO YOU KNOW...

PERFECT CIRCLE **X-90** PISTON RINGS CAN CHANGE DIAMETER **50** TIMES A SECOND? THEY ARE THE **ONLY** PISTON RINGS WITH PATENTED SUPER-RESILIENT, DOUBLE-LEAF SPRINGS THAT HOLD THE RINGS FIRMLY AGAINST TAPERED CYLINDER WALLS AT **ALL** SPEEDS. SEE PAGE 41 OF FREE BOOK.

FREE BOOK ANSWERS

OVER 200 LIFE-AND-DEATH QUESTIONS ON SAFE DRIVING AND HOW TO DOUBLE THE LIFE OF YOUR CAR BY PROPER CARE. MORE THAN 100,000 MOTOR-ISTS HAVE ALREADY SENT FOR THIS VALUABLE AND HELPFUL BOOK. SEND COUPON **NOW** FOR YOUR FREE COPY!

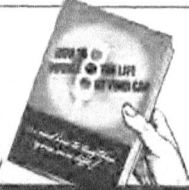

PERFECT CIRCLE
Piston Rings

FILL OUT AND MAIL COUPON — The Perfect Circle Co., Hagerstown, Ind., or Toronto, Can.
Please send me your new book, How to Double the Life of Your Car, and information on my specific model of car or truck. I have filled in each line carefully.

Make of Car or Truck_____ Model No._____ Yr.__ No. Cyl.___ Mileage____

Complaint_____ My Name_____

Dealer's Name_____ My Address_____

His Address_____ City_____ State____

Be sure to give name of garage, mechanic, or car dealer.

Trade-mark Registered   Copyright 1938, The Perfect Circle Company

Perfect Circle piston rings

"It's a beauty, dad! Everyone says it's the best looking car on the street!"

CHEVROLET

People everywhere *are* saying that Chevrolet is the style sensation of 1938. Doubtless you have noticed its distinctive modern beauty yourself. Long, low, massive—a luxury car if ever there was one—it wins a tribute of admiration from every eye, a word of praise from every lip, when finished in any one of the rich, alluring colors Chevrolet is offering. *You'll be ahead with a Chevrolet* . . in style, in features, in performance, in economy . . for the crown of value belongs to *the car that is complete!*

CHEVROLET MOTOR DIVISION, *General Motors Sales Corporation*, DETROIT, MICHIGAN

You'll be AHEAD with a CHEVROLET!
THE CAR THAT IS COMPLETE

MODERN-MODE STYLING

PERFECTED HYDRAULIC BRAKES

GENUINE KNEE-ACTION*

ALL-SILENT ALL-STEEL BODIES

VALVE-IN-HEAD ENGINE

FISHER NO DRAFT VENTILATION

*On Master De Luxe models only.

Chevrolet   General Motors

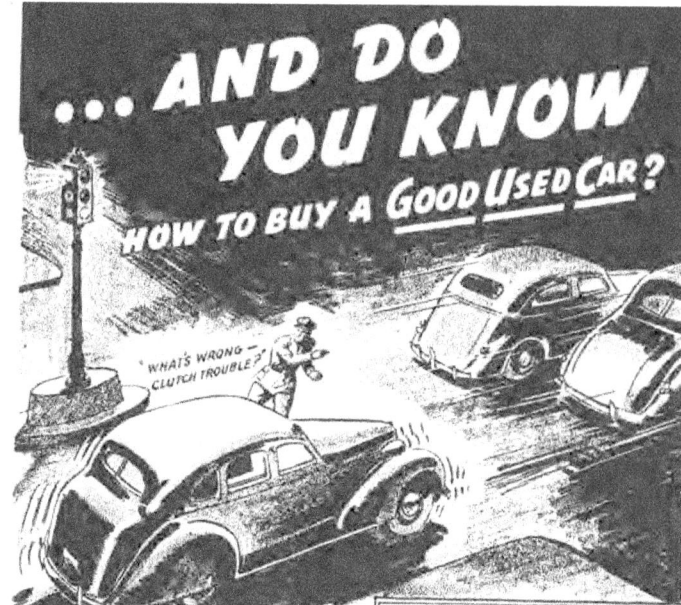

...AND DO YOU KNOW
HOW TO BUY A GOOD USED CAR?

"WHAT'S WRONG? CLUTCH TROUBLE?"

DO YOU KNOW...
HOW TO TELL IF A CAR HAS A
WORN CLUTCH?
THE CLUTCH ON THE AVERAGE USED CAR HAS BEEN ENGAGED AND DISENGAGED OVER **250,000** TIMES! LEARN HOW RELIABLE USED CAR DEALERS TEST FOR WORN CLUTCHES. SEE PAGE 23 OF FREE BOOK.

"BEWARE OF OIL PUMPERS"

DO YOU KNOW.. MANY CARS ARE TRADED IN BECAUSE THEY **PUMP OIL** AND HAVE LOST THEIR POWER? MAKE SURE THAT THE CAR YOU BUY HAS BEEN RECONDITIONED WITH PERFECT CIRCLE **X-90** PISTON RINGS. SEND FOR FREE BOOK.

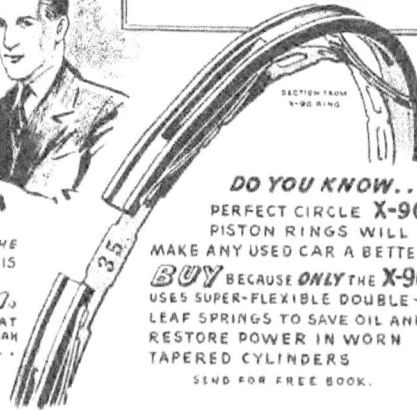

SECTION FROM X-90 RING

INSIST ... THAT THE
USED CAR YOU BUY CARRIES THIS PERFECT CIRCLE **WINDSHIELD EMBLEM,** IT IS YOUR **GUARANTEE** THAT THE BEST PISTON RINGS MONEY CAN BUY HAVE BEEN INSTALLED ....
SEND FOR FREE BOOK.

DO YOU KNOW...
PERFECT CIRCLE **X-90** PISTON RINGS WILL MAKE ANY USED CAR A BETTER **BUY** BECAUSE **ONLY** THE **X-90** USES SUPER-FLEXIBLE DOUBLE-LEAF SPRINGS TO SAVE OIL AND RESTORE POWER IN WORN TAPERED CYLINDERS
SEND FOR FREE BOOK.

FREE BOOK GIVES INSIDE USED CAR FACTS!
THIS AMAZING BOOKLET REVEALS, FOR THE FIRST TIME, FACTS OF VITAL INTEREST TO USED CAR BUYERS. WRITTEN BY PERFECT CIRCLE ENGINEERS, IT HELPS YOU BUY LIKE AN EXPERT. IF YOU'RE TRADING OR RECONDITIONING YOUR CAR, **SEND FOR THIS MONEY-SAVING BOOK NOW. IT'S FREE!**

PERFECT CIRCLE
Piston Rings

FILL OUT AND MAIL COUPON—The Perfect Circle Co., Hagerstown, Ind., or Toronto, Can.
Please send me your free book, How to Buy a Good Used Car.   CB-27-60

I now own a _____ Model No. _____ Yr. _____ No. Cyl. _____ Mileage _____

Dealer's Name _____   My Name _____

His Address _____   My Address _____

City _____ State _____   City _____ State _____
Trade-mark Registered   Copyright 1940, The Perfect Circle Company

Perfect Circle piston rings

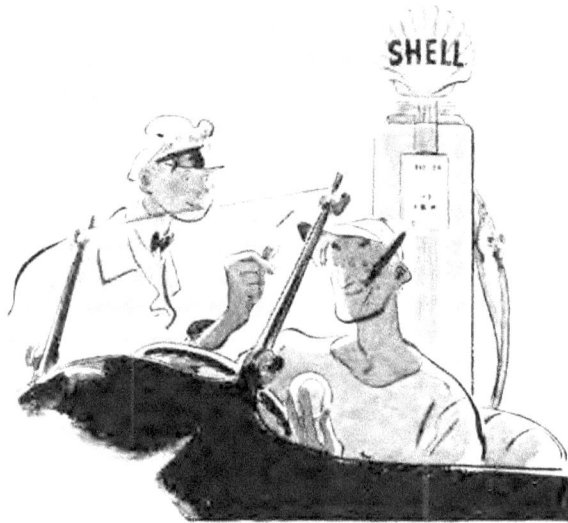

"Gee!" says *this southpaw*

It's the day after Lefty Mason clinches the pennant by shutting out Ford's Bluff in our Three Mountains League, an' the town's still going nuts. The big lug is a *hero*—an' maybe he don't know it!

"Lefty," I says, as he pulls into my place, "let me be the first to—"

"Nuttin' at all—nuttin' at all," he says lightin' a seegar as long as your arm.

Well, a customer's a customer even though he's a swell-headed ballplayer, so I give him the works about Golden Shell Oil. "Lefty," I says, "this Golden Shell goes to work on your engine, when you start, faster'n that speed ball o' yours."

"Gee!" says this guy who is as crazy as most lefthanders. "It's *tough*, too, for steady driving," I go on, "tougher than tryin' to hit that out-drop you feed 'em."

"Yea-a-ah," says the pride of the Blue Sox.

"It's only 25¢ a quart—a bargain, Lefty," I reminds him.

"Put it in," says Lefty, a wild look in his eye. "And give me an extra quart *loose*. I got an idee fer the play-off."

Screwy? Let me tell you what he done—he lubricated the ball with Golden Shell Oil! No hits, no runs, no errors!

Sincerely,

Your Shell Dealer

Shell gasoline

Diamond T truck

From Under The Sea —Longer Life For Your Battery

—in the superpowered Double Eagle 125!

Now—Goodyear's completely new Double Eagle 125 battery has the same heat-, acid- and shock-resistant Microporous Rubber Separators as those used in the U. S. Navy's rugged batteries! Together with a special glass fiber insulation, these separators make Double Eagle 125 longer-lived, more efficient, too.

In fact, every part of this revolutionary battery is built for heavy duty: There's 67% more starting stamina than standard equipment batteries — 39% greater power reserve to operate all accessories—and its new blue and yellow Polystyrene case is twice as strong as the finest rubber case!

Ask your Goodyear Dealer about this superpowered Double Eagle 125, soon. Goodyear, Battery Dept., Akron 16, Ohio.

GOODYEAR

DRY PROOF DOUBLE EAGLE BATTERY

Goodyear battery

DON'T BE PUSHED AROUND THIS WINTER!

Your car will start fast with patented
FIVE-RIB CHAMPION SPARK PLUGS!

Whatever the weather . . . just touch the starter and your full-firing Champion Spark Plugs go to work!

Champion's exclusive FIVE-RIB insulator design protects you against electrical "flash-over" due to dampness — a major cause of hard starting.

Compare a FIVE-RIB Champion with an ordinary spark plug and you'll see why.

Champion's insulating surface is greater because of its ribbed construction. Exterior electricity is diverted and spent before it can short out a damp plug. Tests prove this gives you as much as forty percent more protection than smooth insulator types under the same conditions.

Get the jump on winter now. Let your Champion dealer install a set of FIVE-RIB Champions when your car has its winter change-over.

You'll get going, and get where you're going, with Champions!

CHAMPION SPARK PLUG COMPANY, TOLEDO 1, OHIO

INSIST ON FIVE-RIB
CHAMPIONS

Champion spark plugs

for SAFETY'S SAKE

WAGNER
AUTHORIZED
HYDRAULIC
Brake Service
GENUINE LOCKHEED PARTS

Have the hydraulic brakes on your car checked and serviced by a station that displays this sign

It is economical and wise to make sure that the hydraulic brake system of your car is kept filled to the proper level with genuine Wagner Lockheed Hydraulic Brake Fluid.

Drive into any authorized service station that displays the Wagner red, white and blue sign. A trained mechanic will quickly check your car.

If fluid is needed—genuine Wagner Lockheed Fluid is the answer... If new parts are required—genuine Wagner Lockheed Parts assure the kind of brake performance the automobile manufacturer had in mind when designing the car.

For safety's sake—look up the nearest authorized station TODAY.

LOCKHEED
HYDRAULIC
BRAKE
FLUID

AUTOMOTIVE PARTS DIVISION

Wagner Electric Corporation
6400 Plymouth Ave., St. Louis, U. S. A.

Wagner Hydraulic Brake Service

There are only 11 months in your "Year to pay"

Stanley Walton is glad to hear what a generous trade-in allowance Dealer John Creighton of Ossining, N.Y., is making because of the extra-good care he's given his car

INCREASING the trade-in value of your old car is like cutting out one of the monthly installments. And that's just what you can do by lubricating your car with MARFAK. Here's what Mr. Creighton says on the subject:

"A used car kept in tip-top mechanical condition with MARFAK is easily disposed of. That's why MARFAK users can generally figure on a good break from our appraisers."

MARFAK lasts longer because it is made with heavy bodied oils. Unlike ordinary greases made with light bodied oils, MARFAK resists every kind of use and abuse regardless of driving conditions, of weather, of speed.

Go to your Texaco Dealer today. Let him Marfak your car. Remember, this is no ordinary grease job. It includes many additional services, executed by specially trained men using special equipment. And the cost is surprisingly low.

DON'T SAY "GREASE IT"

Let us MARFAK your car

Copyright 1938, The Texas Company

Marfak

SIMONIZ GIVES A CAR SEX-APPEAL

MAKES ALL FINISHES STAY BEAUTIFUL

Everybody admires a Simonized car! And you'll be surprised how quickly and easily you can give your car this irresistible beauty with the world-famous Simoniz and Simoniz Kleener. They are, without question, the greatest products ever developed for cleaning and protecting all automobile finishes. Simoniz Kleener thoroughly cleans and restores the lustre to your car in one easy operation. Simoniz gives protection the finish must have to last longer and stay beautiful. It alone contains a secret ingredient, which keeps the elements from dulling and eventually destroying the lacquer or enamel. So, to save your car's beauty, don't delay Simonizing it! Get the long-lasting Simoniz and the wonderful Simoniz Kleener today! Always insist on them for your car!

MOTORISTS WISE
SIMONIZ

Simoniz car polish

PRESENTING – 3 New Silver Streaks for 1939

PAY LESS FOR A PONTIAC
THIS YEAR — AND GET MORE!

AMERICA'S FINEST
LOW-PRICED CAR

FINER THAN EVER IN
EVERY WAY AND NOTABLY
LOWER IN PRICE!

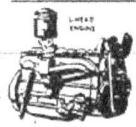

Pontiac

INDEX

www.ingramcontent.com/pod-product-compliance
Lightning Source LLC
Chambersburg PA
CBHW081426090426
42740CB00017B/3191